THE UNZIPPED GUIDES™
for everything you forgot to learn in school

Peterson's

Speeches & Presentations
UNZIPPED

PETERSON'S

A ⓝelnet COMPANY

PETERSON'S

A ⓝelnet COMPANY

About Peterson's, a Nelnet company

Peterson's (www.petersons.com) is a leading provider of education information and advice, with books and online resources focusing on education search, test preparation, and financial aid. Its Web site offers searchable databases and interactive tools for contacting educational institutions, online practice tests and instruction, and planning tools for securing financial aid. Peterson's serves 110 million education consumers annually.

For more information, contact Peterson's, 2000 Lenox Drive, Lawrenceville, NJ 08648; 800-338-3282; or find us on the World Wide Web at: www.petersons.com/about.

© 2007 Peterson's, a Nelnet company

Editor: Fern A. Oram; Production Editor: Bernadette Webster; Manufacturing Manager: Ray Golaszewski; Composition Manager: Gary Rozmierski

ISBN-13: 978-0-7689-2486-2
ISBN-10: 0-7689-2486-3

Printed in the United States of America

10 9 8 7 6 5 4 3 2 1   09 08 07

First Edition

MORE UNZIPPED GUIDES

CONTENTS

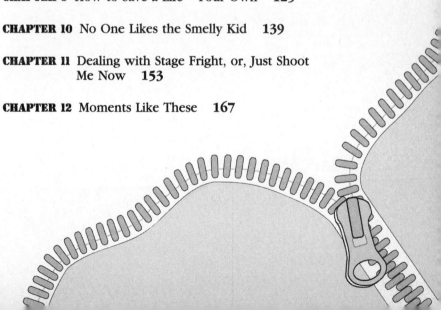

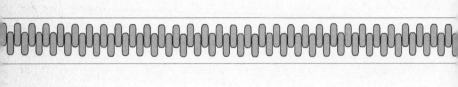

CHAPTER 1

Super Models

EVERYONE'S HEARD THIS old saying:

> *It's not what you say; it's how you say it.*

Well, no.

Successful public speakers know it's *what* you say as well as *how* you say it. Both content and form matter. No matter how polished your presentation, your speech will sink faster than the *Titanic* if you've got nothing of value to say. But the inverse is true as well. Even the best speech can be marred by an inept delivery. As a result, you need to learn how to write a solid speech, as well as how to deliver one with confidence and ease. That's the "unzipped" part of this book.

You'll read classic, as well as contemporary, speeches and learn why they're so successful. Then you'll learn how to craft a speech to suit your personal style, audience, and purpose. We'll teach you how to become comfortable speaking in public and how to use body language, along with your voice, to convey your ideas with clarity and class. Let's start unzipping.

THE IMPORTANCE OF SPEAKING IN PUBLIC WITH CONFIDENCE

The value of being able to stand up and speak without ramming your foot down your throat is nothing new. In fact, the importance

WORDS UNZIPPED

Oratory: A term used to describe the art of public speaking, especially eloquence or skill in public speaking. Here's how it's used in a sentence: "The disgraced politician nonetheless moved the audience to sympathy with his powerful oratory."

of speaking in public stretches back as far as the classical age. The ancient Greeks and Romans recognized that no one is born knowing how to orate—public speaking, like any other skill worth knowing, can be taught and learned.

In ancient Rome, for instance, the art of public speaking was called *Ars Oratoria*. Ancient Roman lawyers and politicians (as well as lawyer and political wannabees) worked to master the skill, as they well recognized its importance in achieving their aims. Since the Greeks had the edge when it came to public speaking, well-to-do Romans sent their sons to Greek tutors to learn to orate. Julius Caesar was a case in point—you don't conquer worlds without knowing how to sway the masses, after all.

Fast forward thousands of years.

In the dark ages—before television, movies, and video games—public speakers were huge draws. They would often widely tour and address large crowds. Some hawked their books while entertaining, most notably Mark Twain and

Charles Dickens. Others hawked their own brand of "snake oil," from patent medicines to patent religions. No matter what they hawked, the good speakers were hugely popular.

WHAT MAKES A GOOD PUBLIC SPEAKER?

Identifying an effective public speaker is like trying to define obscenity. As Supreme Court Justice Potter Stewart declared in his famous ruling: *I shall not today attempt further to define the kinds of material I understand to be embraced [pornography] . . . but I know it when I see it.* In the same way, you know a great public speaker when you're fortunate enough to hear one, even if you can't put the definition into words. But let's give it a shot. . . .

A great public speaker:

- Is interesting and knowledgeable.

- Suits the message to the audience.

- Uses language skillfully.

- Uses audio-visual aids effectively.

- Can be heard easily, even from the back of the room.

- Speaks at the appropriate rate of speed.

- Forges a bond with the audience.

- Is well prepared.

- Is well-groomed.

- Is self-confident.

- Knows when the speech is over.

Let's look at these qualities in more detail.

MORE TO UNZIP

Mark Twain (which was the pen name of Samuel Langhorne Clemens, 1835–1910) gave speeches throughout Egypt and Europe, as well as America. He rocketed to fame with his first collection of travel letters, *The Innocents Abroad*, published in 1869. The book is still worth a careful read as a sterling example of good writing, especially as it pertains to using language to both convey your message and entertain your audience.

Interesting and Knowledgeable

The speaker conveys a message that you want to hear—even if you didn't think you wanted to learn about the subject or even be present at the speech. An effective public speaker, as with any talented performer, makes time seem to go fast. You get caught up in the speech. You find yourself moved by the speaker's words, your senses stirred. In part, this is because the speech is well-written, with a clear method of organization. It's also because the speaker is knowledgeable and comes across as an expert on the topic. Impressive public speakers make sense because they have the facts, details, and examples to back up their thoughts.

Suits the Message to the Audience

Great speakers don't pander to their audiences, but neither do they insult them. With a hostile audience, it's especially important to win people over to your side.

WORDS UNZIPPED

Rhetoric: The art of influencing the thought and conduct of an audience. Today, we usually take the term to mean the ability to use language effectively, especially when applied to the art of making persuasive speeches.

Uses Language Skillfully

A superb speaker understands the effects of diction, parallel structure, alliteration, tone, and other literary and poetic devices. Let's look at a brief illustration from one of the masters of public speaking, Abraham Lincoln. His *Gettysburg Address,* a funeral oration that he delivered November 19, 1863, remains a benchmark for brilliant public speaking. Lincoln delivered his memorable eulogy in fewer than 280 words. Brevity really is the soul of wit.

This is Lincoln's speech. Read it through all the way, savoring its effect. Then read it again, this time following the callouts to find the elements of effective public speaking.

[1] *Four score and seven years ago our fathers brought forth on this continent, a new nation,* [2] *conceived in liberty,* and [1] *dedicated to the proposition that all men are created equal.*

Now we are engaged in a great civil war, testing whether that nation, or any nation [2] *so conceived and so dedicated, can long endure. We are met on a great battlefield of that war. We have come to dedicate a portion of that field, as a final resting place for those who here gave their lives that that nation might live. It is altogether* [2] *fitting and proper that we should do this.*

But in a larger sense, [2] *we cannot dedicate—we cannot consecrate—we cannot hallow—this ground. The brave men,* [2] *living and dead, who struggled here, have consecrated it, far above our* [3] *poor power to add or detract. The world will* [2] *little note, nor long remember, what we say here, but it can never forget what they did here.* [4] *It is for us the living, rather, to be dedicated here to the unfinished work which they who fought here have thus far so nobly advanced. It is rather for us to be here dedicated to the great task remaining before us—that from these honored* [3] *dead we take increased* [3] *devotion to that cause for which they gave the last full measure of devotion—that we here highly resolve that these dead shall not have died in vain—that this nation, under God, shall have a new birth of freedom—and that government* [2] *of the people, by the people, for the people, shall not perish from the earth.*

[1] *Diction* is word choice. Lincoln uses formal, elevated words and Biblical diction to capture the solemnity and holiness of the occasion. He could have said "87 years ago" instead, but it wouldn't have had the same effect.

[2] *Parallel structure* is matching grammatical structures. Parallelism makes the speech flow musically.

[3] *Alliteration* is the repetition of initial consonant sounds in several words in a sentence. Writers use alliteration to create musical effects, link related ideas, stress certain words, or mimic specific sounds.

[4] *Tone* is the mood or feeling you get from the speech. The tone here is formal, dignified, and solemn, as befitting the occasion.

Uses Audio-Visual Aids Effectively

Whether it's low-tech posters and chalkboard or high-tech PowerPoint and TelePrompTer, the speaker handles his equipment comfortably. The audio-visuals add to the presentation, rather than detract from it.

MORE TO UNZIP

According to urban legend, Lincoln hastily scrawled his speech on an envelope on the way to the battleground. Not so. Rather, he carefully crafted his speech, making only some last-minute revisions. Ironically, Lincoln didn't think that his speech had been a success. The newspapers concurred, largely ignoring his brief remarks. However, the keynote speaker that day at Gettysburg, Edward Everett, recognized that Lincoln had made history by delivering words that would echo through the ages.

Heard Easily, Even from the Back of the Room

No matter how good a speech may seem, it's a disaster unless the audience can hear it. With today's sophisticated microphones, there's no excuse for inaudible speeches.

Speaks at the Appropriate Rate of Speed

Nervous speakers tend to race through their scripts, no doubt hoping to end the experience sooner. If you wanted to go to the races, you'd be there.

Forges a Bond with the Audience

Great speakers make frequent eye contact and use pauses strategically so the audience feels that they are speaking right to them.

Well-Prepared

Who wants to see a speaker fumble with papers and words? Who wants to listen to speakers apologize for not knowing their speech?

Well-Groomed

Well, folks, we shouldn't have to bring up s-w-e-a-t, but the lights are "bright on stage." Add a dash of stage fright, and it's no wonder that all the celebs are getting Botox injections in their armpits to avoid those tell-tale sweat stains.

Self-Confident

Fabulous speakers command center stage and enjoy it. These speakers are relaxed and appear delighted to be addressing the audience. As a result, audiences find the speaker's enthusiasm contagious. If the speaker feels any stage fright, it's surely not being conveyed to the audience.

Last but Not Least

Effective public speakers *know when to stop speaking.* It ain't over till the fat lady sings, as they say at the opera, but you want to leave the stage before they drag you off with a hook.

LEARN FROM THE MASTERS

Want to be a better golfer? Watch how the experts swing. Want to be a better cook? Watch how the experts sauté. Want to be a better public speaker? Watch how the experts speak and stand. Listen carefully to their words. Watch their posture. Check out their hand gestures, facial expressions, and eye contact. Look at the following list of superb public speakers. You don't have to agree with their politics or admire their peccadilloes. Just watch and listen to them speak every chance you get. You can see the dead guys on movies and TV shows; the live guys appear frequently, well, in-person (as well as on TV). You'll notice that many of the people on this list are professional performers. That's no coincidence—public speaking is a performance.

Speaker	Day Job
Winston Churchill	Great Britain's prime minister during World War II
Bill Clinton	Politician

Speaker	Day Job
Bill Cosby	Actor, educator
Mario Cuomo	Politician
Ellen Degeneres	Stand-up comedian, talk-show host
Dr. Martin Luther King Jr.	Civil rights leader, minister
Jay Leno	Stand-up comedian, talk-show host
David Letterman	Stand-up comedian, talk-show host
Franklin Delano Roosevelt	America's president during the Depression and World War II
Jerry Seinfeld	Stand-up comedian, actor

MODEL SPEECH: WINSTON CHURCHILL'S "BLOOD, SWEAT, AND TEARS"

In addition to being a masterful leader, Winston Churchill (1874–1965) was a brilliant writer. Churchill delivered one of the most rousing call-to-arms ever spoken on May 13, 1940. An excerpt follows.

. . . we are in the preliminary phase of one of the greatest battles in history. We are in action at many other points—in Norway and in Holland—and we have to be prepared in the Mediterranean. The air battle is continuing, and many preparations have to be made here at home.

In this crisis I think I may be pardoned if I do not address the House at any length today, and I hope that any of my friends and colleagues or former colleagues who are affected by the political reconstruction will make all allowances for any lack of ceremony with which it has been necessary to act.

I say to the House as I said to ministers who have joined this government, I have nothing to offer but blood, toil, tears, and

MORE TO UNZIP

Famous classical orators include Demosthenes, Claudius Aelianus, Cicero (the defender of the Roman Republic), Cato the Elder, Paul of Tarsos, Peter the Hermit, Marcus Fabius Quintilianus, and Seneca the Rhetorician. Unfortunately, they didn't leave any audio or videotape.

sweat. We have before us an ordeal of the most grievous kind. We have before us many, many months of struggle and suffering.

You ask, what is our policy? I say it is to wage war by land, sea, and air. War with all our might and with all the strength God has given us, and to wage war against a monstrous tyranny never surpassed in the dark and lamentable catalogue of human crime. That is our policy.

You ask, what is our aim? I can answer in one word. It is victory. Victory at all costs—Victory in spite of all terrors—Victory, however long and hard the road may be, for without victory there is no survival.

Let that be realized. No survival for the British Empire, no survival for all that the British Empire has stood for, no survival for the urge, the impulse of the ages, that mankind shall move forward toward his goal.

I take up my task in buoyancy and hope. I feel sure that our cause will not be suffered to fail among men. I feel entitled at this juncture, at this time, to claim the aid of all and to say, "Come then, let us go forward together with our united strength."

CHAPTER 2

One, Two, Three, Speak!

PEOPLE TEND TO think in threes: Three Stooges, Three Amigos, Three Kings, Three Blind Mice—you get the idea. If you break out in a cold sweat when it comes to speaking in public, not to worry. After all, there are only three basic kinds of speeches that you'll be asked to deliver: *informative speeches, persuasive speeches,* and *entertaining speeches.* In this chapter, you'll learn about each one. This will make it a lot easier for you to create a speech to match your audience and occasion.

LET ME INFORM YOU

Informative speeches are just what their name trumpets: speeches that give information. These speeches explain, report, describe, clarify, define, and demonstrate. Here are some commonplace types of informative speeches:

- Court testimony

- Incident or accident reports

- Process explanations

- Job training sessions

- School lectures

- Job candidate interviews

- Progress reports

- Directions

Now let's look at four ways to make these speeches sparkle.

Organize Carefully

There are several different ways to organize your information. Always choose the method that best suits your audience, purpose, and topic. Below are the top methods for organizing informative speeches, the types of informative speeches that best suit each method, and some sample topics so you can see how to apply these methods of organization.

Method of Organization	Type of Informative Speech	Sample Topic
Alphabetical order	Job training sessions	Introduction to the company's product line
Cause and effect	Incident and/or accident reports	Court testimony about a car accident
Chronological order	Directions, process explanations	Directions for preparing for a medical test
Numerical order	Process explanations, job training	How to set up a computer, how to bake a cake

Method of Organization	Type of Informative Speech	Sample Topic
Problem-solution order	School lecture, job training	Troubleshooting a nonfunctional machine
Spatial order (order of space)	Descriptions of places or things	Describing a new office building or dorm
Topical (subject) order	School lectures	The three branches of the federal government

The arrangement of information on this chart isn't carved in stone, so feel free to mix and match. It's worth saying again: Always choose the method that best suits your audience, purpose, and topic.

Cover Three Points

Yes, we're back at that magic number again. As a general rule, include no more than three main points in an informative speech. Here's a sample outline:

    I. Introduction: Tell your audience what you are going to say.
   II. First main idea
  III. Second main idea
  IV. Third main idea
   V. Conclusion: Tell your audience what you said.

Use Details

Some informative speeches are mind-numbingly tedious, as you no doubt experienced at the hands of Dr. Schmendrick in freshman World Civilization 101. But not *your* informative speeches! Your informative speeches will sizzle! Your audience will be at the edges

MORE TO UNZIP

The number *three* has many superstitions swirling around it. Good and bad luck is said to come in threes. The number three is considered good luck in Chinese culture because it sounds like the word "alive," but in Vietnamese culture, it's bad luck to take a photo with three people in it.

of their seats, awaiting your next pearl of wisdom. How can you make an informative topic that's as dry as a stale rice cake as juicy as a richly marbled steak?

- Know your topic.
  Informative speeches require an in-depth level of knowledge to convey facts that people really need.

- Rehearse thoroughly so you don't have to read from a text.
  Watching a speaker with his head buried in the textbook, droning on, is about as exciting as watching paint dry. Wait—watching paint dry is more exciting.

- Spice up informative speeches and make your point with descriptive details, vivid words, and accurate facts.

Just because informative speeches aren't as emotional as persuasive speeches or as knee-slappin' humorous as entertaining speeches doesn't mean they have to be dull. Just the opposite, which you know if you've ever had a gifted teacher.

Integrate Visuals

Further, since a picture is worth a thousand words, you'll want to illustrate your informative speeches with heaps and heaps of visuals. Use carefully-chosen graphs, charts, posters, handouts, manipulatives (such as models), chalk talks, flip charts, maps, photographs, videotapes, audiotapes, slides, PowerPoint, and so on. All these audio-visual aids will help you convey your point in a clear and interesting way.

MODEL INFORMATIVE SPEECH:
CLASS LECTURE

Here's the introduction to a class lecture.

William Faulkner's The Sound and the Fury *is ranked as a masterpiece for its style and content. Faulkner used stream of consciousness, interior monologues, discontinuous time, fragmented chronological order, multiple narrators, complex allusions, and allegory. Its content concerns Southern memory, reality, and myth, with the focus on honor and sin, as seen through the tragic decline of the mythical Compson family. The novel tells the story through four different viewpoints: the three Compson brothers— Benjy, Quentin, and Jason—and their black servant, Dilsey.*

The first section, April 7, 1928, is told from the point of view of Benjy Compson, a mentally retarded 33-year-old man. The second section, June 2, 1910, tells the same story from Quentin's point of

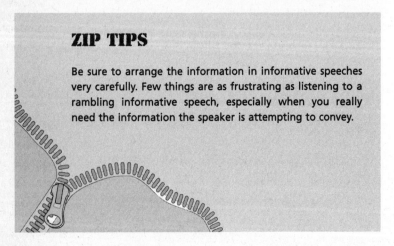

ZIP TIPS

Be sure to arrange the information in informative speeches very carefully. Few things are as frustrating as listening to a rambling informative speech, especially when you really need the information the speaker is attempting to convey.

view on the day he commits suicide. A student at Harvard, he is obsessed with the traditional Southern concepts of womanhood, virginity, and honor as they relate to his sister, Caddy, pregnant outside of marriage. The third section, April 6, 1928, narrated by Jason, takes place on Good Friday. Jason is livid because his niece, Caddy (his sister's daughter), has taken $7,000 that he thinks is his. The final section, April 8, 1928, is told from the omniscient viewpoint. There are two main plot lines: Jason trying to recover the $7,000 and Dilsey's attendance at an Easter church service.

LET ME CONVINCE YOU

Persuasive speeches aim to move an audience to belief or action. Here are some commonplace types of persuasive speeches:

- Appeals for funds

- Apologies for public misconduct

- Election speeches

- Nominations

- Job interviews

- Sales presentations

You have three main ways to persuade:

1. Appeal to ethics (values, character, and reputation)

2. Appeal to emotion

3. Appeal to reason

Aristotle put it this way: *Of the modes of persuasion furnished by the spoken word there are three kinds. The first kind depends on the personal character of the speaker [ethos]; the second on putting the audience into a certain frame of mind [pathos]; the third on the proof, or apparent proof, provided by the words of the speech itself [logos].*

You can combine these appeals to achieve your purpose. Choose the method(s) that work best with your purpose, topic, and

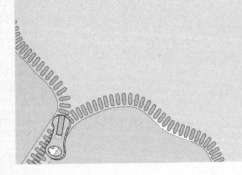

ZIP TIPS

Wikipedia.org, the online encyclopedia written by anyone with access to a computer, is a tempting resource. Resist the temptation, just as you would shun a peanut-butter-and-pickle sandwich. Since anyone and everyone can post on Wiki, the information is not reliable. If you absolutely positively MUST use Wiki, be sure to verify the information you find there in at least one other reliable source, such as a print encyclopedia, an almanac, or a scholarly reference book.

audience. For instance, public-service television commercials for anti-smoking and anti-drunk driving campaigns often appeal to emotion. That's because ad executives know this is the most effective way to reach their audience. But effective employment interviews appeal to reason and ethics. You'd never whine at an employment interview, "Pleeze gimme this job. I really need this job." Rather, you'd clearly and concisely state specific reasons why you are best suited for the position. That's because you know this method would be most effective in snagging you the job.

Here's how to persuade your audience.

Provide Sufficient Information

Intelligent people are swayed by facts, details, and examples. Ethical speakers use valid proof to make their point. Keep these points in mind as you do your research.

Quality

Use only grade A facts. Double-check them to make sure that you've got all your ducks in a row. Nothing demolishes an argument more effectively than flawed data.

Bias

Recognize that every source has a bias, a slant. For instance, people who read a hunter's magazine will likely feel we should all chow down on Bambi the first chance we get, while a vegan journal would find such a viewpoint abhorrent.

Suitability

No matter how lovely the proof, if it doesn't fit your audience, purpose, and topic, ditch it.

Overcome the Listener's Objections

Rarely is an issue merely one-sided. If it were, there would be no purpose in arguing it. For instance, we all know that leafy green vegetables are good for you and trans fat is bad for you—so why would you argue the opposing side? When you persuade, recognize that the other side has some valid points. Your job is to show that your points are *more* valid.

Start these speeches by stating the opposition's main points. Give them the credit that is their due. Then counter with your own points, which will be much stronger than the opposition's points.

Structure your speech this way:

    I. Introduction: Tell your audience what you are going to say.

    II. Opposition
        A. Their first point
        B. Their second point

    III. Your side
        A. Show why their first point is not valid
        B. Show why their second point is not valid
        C. Your first point
        D. Your strongest point

    IV. Conclusion: Tell your audience what you said.

Speak Fairly and Ethically

Unethical speakers use *logical fallacies* to sway their audience. The following chart shows some of the most common errors in logic. Of course, you'll never use any of these in your speeches. Ever.

Logical Fallacy	Definition	Example
Begging the question	Stating a position that needs to be proven as though it has already been proven and widely accepted	This election's issue is whether Luci deserves another term as student government president after such a disgraceful year in office.
Bogus claims	Promising more than you can deliver	Everyone knows that the cabbage diet will help you lose 15 pounds a week.
False analogies	Making misleading comparisons	School politics is like a baseball game. In baseball, if a player doesn't follow the coach's signals, the player is pulled off the field. So any student leader who doesn't obey the class president should be kicked out of office.

Logical Fallacy	Definition	Example
Loaded terms	Using words that have strong emotional overtones	*regime* rather than *administration*
Oversimplifying the issue	Twisting the truth by presenting too narrow a range of possibilities	Here we have a clear-cut choice between a plan that will result in school-wide catastrophe or a plan that will result in great success in the school and the community.
Backwards reasoning	Confusing cause and effect; before and after	Republicians are always proposing tax increases. Mayor Jones is proposing a tax increase. From this we can conclude that Major Jones is a Republician.

MODEL PERSUASIVE SPEECH: QUEEN ELIZABETH I

Queen Elizabeth I of England (1533–1603) delivered the following speech in 1588, as the British ships prepared to meet the Spanish Armada. The British defeated the Spanish Armada and became the dominant world power, remaining so for centuries. Can we credit Lizzy's speech for the stunning victory? It surely didn't hurt.

My loving people, we have been persuaded by some, that are careful of our safety, to take heed how we commit ourselves to armed multitudes, for fear of treachery; but I assure you, I do not desire to live to distrust my faithful and loving people. Let tyrants fear; I have always so behaved myself that, under God, I have placed my chiefest strength and safeguard in the loyal hearts and good will of my subjects. And therefore I am come amongst you at

MORE TO UNZIP

Queen Elizabeth I, daughter of King Henry VIII and Anne Boleyn, was called the "Virgin Queen" for reasons too obvious to state. Twenty-five years old when she assumed the throne, she ruled England for 44 years until age 69.

this time, not as for my recreation or sport, but being resolved, in the midst and heat of the battle, to live or die amongst you all; to lay down, for my God, and for my kingdom, and for my people, my honor and my blood, even the dust. I know I have but the body of a weak and feeble woman; but I have the heart of a king, and of a king of England, too; and think foul scorn that Parma or Spain, or any prince of Europe, should dare to invade the borders of my realms: to which, rather than any dishonor should grow by me, I myself will take up arms; I myself will be your general, judge, and rewarder of every one of your virtues in the field. I know already, by your forwardness, that you have deserved rewards and crowns; and we do assure you, on the word of a prince, they shall be duly paid you. In the mean my lieutenant general shall be in my stead, than whom never prince commanded a more noble and worthy subject; not doubting by your obedience to my general, by your concord in the camp, and by your valor in the field, we shall shortly have a famous victory over the enemies of my God, of my kingdom, and of my people.

LET ME ENTERTAIN YOU

Entertaining speeches are like social glue because they cement relationships between people and establish the speaker (that's you) as the cool kid on the block. Here are some commonplace entertaining speeches.

- Addresses of welcome

- Introductions

- Dedications of buildings, etc.

- Eulogies

- Toasts

- Roasts

Here's what you need to know to be the life of the party.

Deliver a Clear, Central Theme

It's tempting to get up and ramble at these occasions. Not a good move. Instead, prepare these speeches as carefully as you would speeches that inform and those that persuade. Start by deciding on your message, your main idea. Then arrange your speech in a logical way. Here's a sample structure.

ZIP TIPS

The temptation to get loaded to "relax" before a speech is strong. Don't. Ever. Never. You'll think you're Joe Cool. Your audience will realize you're Joe Jerk.

WORDS UNZIPPED

Tone: The writer's attitude toward his or her subject matter. For example, the tone can be angry, bitter, sad, humorous, or frightening.

I. Open with an anecdote, a brief story, or a joke.
II. State your main idea and tie it into the anecdote or joke.
III. Provide additional anecdotes on your main idea.
IV. Restate your main idea. Tell another great anecdote or joke.

Strike the Right Tone

The tone is established by your choice of words, body language, facial expressions, and voice. Unless you're delivering a eulogy, your speech should be optimistic, upbeat, and lively. After all, your purpose is to entertain. Also, keep your speech simple and uncomplicated. No lecture, just fun.

Link Your Speech to the Audience's Needs and Wants

If you've ever lost a loved one, you've likely been interviewed by the person delivering the eulogy. Even if the religious leader knew the departed well, he or she will ask the family for anecdotes to share. That's because religious leaders know that effective eulogies must be precisely tailored to suit the audience. The same is true of all speeches that entertain. Just as religious leaders do at funerals, you can get information by interviewing people.

MODEL ENTERTAINING SPEECH: MARK TWAIN

Here's the beginning of a speech that Mark Twain delivered at The Lotos Club, January 11, 1908.

I wish to begin this time at the beginning, lest I forget it altogether; that is to say, I wish to thank you for this welcome that you are giving, and the welcome which you gave me seven years ago, and which I forgot to thank you for at that time. I also wish to thank you for the welcome you gave me fourteen years ago, which I also forgot to thank you for at the time.

I hope you will continue this custom to give me a dinner every seven years before I join the hosts in the other world—I do not know which world.

Mr. Lawrence and Mr. Porter have paid me many compliments. It is very difficult to take compliments. I do not care whether you deserve the compliments or not, it is just as difficult to take them. The other night I was at the Engineers' Club, and enjoyed the sufferings of Mr. Carnegie. They were complimenting him there; there it was all compliments, and none of them deserved. They say that you cannot live by bread alone, but I can live on compliments.

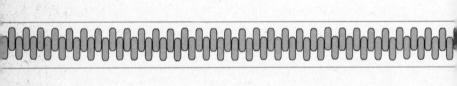

CHAPTER 3

Every Time We Touch

BRITISH PLAYWRIGHT GEORGE Bernard Shaw once said: *Reasonable people adapt themselves to the world. Unreasonable people attempt to adapt the world to themselves.* Nowhere is this truer than when it comes to speeches. To be a powerful public speaker, you have to give the audience what *they* want—not what *you* want. Effective public speaking starts and ends with an in-depth awareness of your audience.

Albert Einstein, a man who knew a thing or two about learning, said: *Example isn't another way to teach; it is the only way to teach.* Taking Einstein's advice to heart, here are two famous speeches to analyze for their audience. As you read each speech, identify each speech's audience. Then decide how the speaker appeals to his audience in each instance.

MODEL SPEECH: PRESIDENT BILL CLINTON, DECEMBER 11, 1998

Clinton delivered this speech just before the House Judiciary Committee voted to pass its first article of impeachment.

Good afternoon.

As anyone close to me knows, for months I have been grappling with how best to reconcile myself to the American people, to acknowledge my own wrongdoing, and still to maintain my focus on the work of the presidency.

WORDS UNZIPPED

Audience: People to whom you are speaking. Your audience can be as small as one person or as large as thousands of people watching you appear on a television show.

Others are presenting my defense on the facts, the law, and the Constitution. Nothing I can say now can add to that.

What I want the American people to know, what I want the Congress to know is that I am profoundly sorry for all I have done wrong in words and deeds. I never should have misled the country, the Congress, my friends, or my family. Quite simply, I gave in to my shame. I have been condemned by my accusers with harsh words.

Mere words cannot fully express the profound remorse I feel for what our country is going through and for what members of both parties in Congress are now forced to deal with. These past months have been a torturous process of coming to terms with what I did. I understand that accountability demands consequences, and I'm prepared to accept them.

Painful as the condemnation of the Congress would be, it would pale in comparison to the consequences of the pain I have caused my family. There is no greater agony. Like anyone who honestly faces the shame of wrongful conduct, I would give anything to go back and undo what I did.

But one of the painful truths I have to live with is the reality that that is simply not possible. An old and dear friend of mine recently sent me the wisdom of a poet who wrote, "The moving finger writes and having writ, moves on. Nor all your piety nor wit shall lure it back to cancel half a line. Nor all your tears wash out a word of it."

So nothing, not piety, nor tears, nor wit, nor torment can alter what I have done. I must make my peace with that.

Meanwhile, I will continue to do all I can to reclaim the trust of the American people and to serve them well.

Clinton's audience was the American people, those who demanded an apology and a public debasement, the acts of contrition required by contemporary American society to forgive our faux pas. Clinton uses an appeal to emotion to move his audience to pity and sympathy. Today, Clinton's reputation shines, partly because of his brilliant speeches at this, the lowest point in his career.

MODEL SPEECH: PRESIDENT FRANKLIN DELANO ROOSEVELT, DECEMBER 8, 1941

Roosevelt delivered this speech the day after the Japanese bombed Pearl Harbor, plunging the United States into World War II.

Mr. Vice President, Mr. Speaker, Members of the Senate, and of the House of Representatives:

Yesterday, December 7th, 1941—a date which will live in infamy—the United States of America was suddenly and deliberately attacked by naval and air forces of the Empire of Japan.

The United States was at peace with that nation and, at the solicitation of Japan, was still in conversation with its government and its emperor looking toward the maintenance of peace in the Pacific.

Indeed, one hour after Japanese air squadrons had commenced bombing in the American island of Oahu, the Japanese ambassador to the United States and his colleague delivered to our Secretary of State a formal reply to a recent American message. And while this reply stated that it seemed useless to continue the existing diplomatic negotiations, it contained no threat or hint of war or of armed attack.

It will be recorded that the distance of Hawaii from Japan makes it obvious that the attack was deliberately planned many days or even weeks ago. During the intervening time, the Japanese government has deliberately sought to deceive the United States by false statements and expressions of hope for continued peace.

The attack yesterday on the Hawaiian islands has caused severe damage to American naval and military forces. I regret to tell you that very many American lives have been lost. In addition,

American ships have been reported torpedoed on the high seas between San Francisco and Honolulu.

Yesterday, the Japanese government also launched an attack against Malaya.

Last night, Japanese forces attacked Hong Kong.

Last night, Japanese forces attacked Guam.

Last night, Japanese forces attacked the Philippine Islands.

Last night, the Japanese attacked Wake Island.

And this morning, the Japanese attacked Midway Island.

Japan has, therefore, undertaken a surprise offensive extending throughout the Pacific area. The facts of yesterday and today speak for themselves. The people of the United States have already formed their opinions and well understand the implications to the very life and safety of our nation.

As commander-in-chief of the Army and Navy, I have directed that all measures be taken for our defense. But always will our whole nation remember the character of the onslaught against us.

No matter how long it may take us to overcome this premeditated invasion, the American people in their righteous might will win through to absolute victory. I believe that I interpret the will of the Congress and of the people when I assert that we will not only *defend ourselves to the uttermost, but will make it very certain that this form of treachery shall never again endanger us.*

Hostilities exist. There is no blinking at the fact that our people, our territory, and our interests are in grave danger.

With confidence in our armed forces, with the unbounding determination of our people, we will gain the inevitable triumph—so help us God.

I ask that the Congress declare that since the unprovoked and dastardly attack by Japan on Sunday, December 7th, 1941, a state of war has existed between the United States and the Japanese empire.

Roosevelt had a primary and a secondary audience. His primary audience was all Americans; his secondary audience was the entire world, waiting for his declaration of war. As a result, this was arguably the most important speech of Roosevelt's entire presidency. Similarly, Roosevelt uses all three appeals. His primary appeals are to reason and ethic; his secondary appeal is to emotion, especially clear in the second half of the speech. Today, Roosevelt's reputation as a first-rate president is secure, partly because of his brilliant speeches at crucial junctures in the twentieth century.

IDENTIFY YOUR AUDIENCE

A carefully-written speech delivered to the "wrong" audience will have the same result as a poorly-written speech given to the "right" audience: Splat! That's the egg smeared all over the speaker's face. The more you know about your audience and their expectations from you, the more effectively you'll be able to write a speech that soars rather than collapses—or explodes.

As you learned from the two model speeches, you can't write or deliver a word of your speech without knowing your audience. You

MORE TO UNZIP

The Japanese launched their surprise attack on the U.S. fleet at Pearl Harbor and the military installation at 6:00 a.m. that Sunday, hitting the base shortly before 8:00 a.m. The damage was significant: 2,403 military personnel and 68 civilians dead; 1,178 wounded; and 5 battleships, 3 cruisers, and 188 planes destroyed.

must do a complete audience analysis before anything else. That said, here's what you have to consider about your prospective audience.

Biases

As you learned in Chapter 2, *bias* is a preconception, a partiality. Bias is not necessarily bad—after all, what could be wrong about favoring Mute Math over Hanson? But as a public speaker, you must be aware of your audience's biases. This can prevent you from giving a speech on the advantages of waging war to a group of pacifists or the wonders of technology to the Amish.

Number of People in the Audience

Size *does* matter. Is the audience large or small in number?

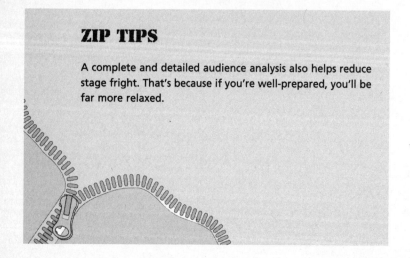

ZIP TIPS

A complete and detailed audience analysis also helps reduce stage fright. That's because if you're well-prepared, you'll be far more relaxed.

Venue

Where will you be speaking and how is the room laid out? The room layout has a significant impact on your presentation. For instance, will you be standing on a stage, at a podium, or at a desk? Will you have access to technology if you require it?

Level of Knowledge

How much does your audience know? Their level of knowledge determines your diction (word choice), allusions (references to well-known people, places, and works of culture), sentence length, and amount of detail.

Also be very sure to find out how much they know about your topic. For instance, you would craft a very different speech about collectibles to an audience of antique dealers than you would to a group of IRS agents.

Attitude toward You

Your audience can be hostile, welcoming, somewhere in between, or neutral. Their attitude may depend on something as solid as your reputation or something as silly as your gender. If you're the first woman to break into the all-men's-cigar-smoking-strip-club, you'll likely not to be embraced with open arms. Especially if you brought a lawsuit to gain membership to the club.

Attitude toward Your Topic and Speech

Will your audience welcome listening to you or do they resent being forced to attend? A group of high school students might be delighted to listen to your speech on drunk driving if only for the chance to miss a class, while teachers are likely to resent the time you're taking away from their classroom instruction.

Your Place on the Agenda

As you analyze your audience, also consider your place on the agenda. For instance, are you the first speaker or the last? If you're the first, you've got a hefty advantage because your audience is fresh and likely more receptive. Also, if you're first, you're not following anyone else, be that speaker suave or stinky. If you're last on the bill, your audience is likely tired and ready to go home.

Average Age of Audience Members

We're all concerned with different things at different stages of our life. High school kids have rarely given a thought to pensions, retirement, and health care; people age 45–55 think of little else.

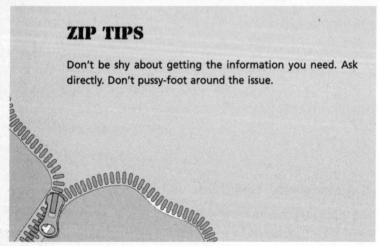

ZIP TIPS

Don't be shy about getting the information you need. Ask directly. Don't pussy-foot around the issue.

Know the age of the people you'll be addressing so you can tailor your speech to their needs and wants.

Life would be easy if everyone cared . . . but they don't, so you have to make them love you. You can't win their undying devotion until you know what they need and want. As a result, ask your audience what they need—and then give it to them.

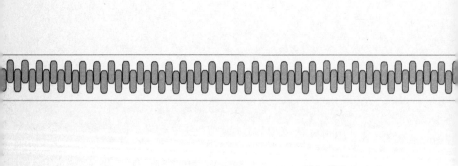

CHAPTER 4

Getting It Together

Q **UESTION:** What is the purpose of every single speech you will ever give? Check one.

[ ] To entertain

[ ] To inform

[ ] To persuade

[ ] To communicate

A **NSWER:** It's the last choice—to communicate.

Whether you're entertaining, informing, or persuading your audience, your primary job is to communicate your ideas and your message clearly and directly. The best way to achieve your goal is to organize your speech carefully.

In this chapter, you'll learn different ways to organize your speeches. Happily, there are many ways to do that. Sadly, we can't cover them all. But following are the most useful methods of speech organization. Again, always choose the method that best suits your audience, purpose, and topic.

CAUSE-AND-EFFECT ORGANIZATION

A *cause* is why something happens; the *effect* is the result. Causes lead to events or results; effects result from causes. The process looks like this:

Cause	Effect
You drink a double espresso at 9:00 p.m.	You can't get to sleep until 3:00 a.m.

Often, a cause can have multiple effects. Likewise, an effect can have multiple causes. Here's a sample.

Cause	Effects
You give a training session at work.	• Employees are better trained. • Work is accomplished faster and easier. • You receive a raise.

To make your speeches easier to understand, start with the causes and then present the effects. Your speech can have one main cause and effect, or multiple ones. As you research ideas and plan your speech, organize your notes on a chart like this one.

Causes	Effects

Cause-and-effect structure tends to be especially effective with persuasive speeches because it helps you present compelling examples and build logic. Nonetheless, this method of organization can be used with any type of speech.

MODEL CAUSE-AND-EFFECT SPEECH: MARK TWAIN

Twain delivered this speech in London in 1907 to receive an honor. As you read, notice the cause-and-effect organization.

My books have had effects, and very good ones, too, here and there, and some others not so good. There is no doubt about that. But I remember one monumental instance of it years and years ago. Professor Norton, of Harvard, was over here, and when he came back to Boston I went out with Howells to call on him. Norton was allied in some way by marriage with Darwin.

ZIP TIPS

Even with complex topics, avoid presenting too many causes and effects. Keep the number manageable, so your audience can follow your logic.

Mr. Norton was very gentle in what he had to say, and almost delicate, and he said: "Mr. Clemens, I have been spending some time with Mr. Darwin in England, and I should like to tell you something connected with that visit. You were the object of it, and I myself would have been very proud of it, but you may not be proud of it. At any rate, I am going to tell you what it was, and to leave to you to regard it as you please. Mr. Darwin took me up to his bedroom and pointed out certain things there—pitcher-plants, and so on, that he was measuring and watching from day to day—and he said: 'The chambermaid is permitted to do what she pleases in this room, but she must never touch those plants and never touch those books on that table by that candle. With those books I read myself to sleep every night.' Those were your own books." I said: "There is no question to my mind as to whether I should regard that as a compliment or not. I do regard it as a very great compliment and a very high honor that that great mind, laboring for the whole human race, should rest itself on my books. I am proud that he should read himself to sleep with them."

CHRONOLOGICAL ORGANIZATION

Chronological order is the order of time. It's an especially effective method of organization for stories, anecdotes, and informative speeches because it helps you create suspense and build to a punch line. It's the only way to tell an effective joke.

Chronological order is the only method for *process analysis* speeches. Often called "how-to" speeches, process analysis describes a sequence of actions by which something is done or made. Process analysis speeches often provide step-by-step instructions.

As you write, link your ideas with time-order words to make your story easier to follow. You can also use dates and times. Here are some examples of time-order transition words.

- First
- Second
- Third
- Next
- Then

- Last
- Finally
- After
- Subsequently
- Ultimately
- Previously

As you write your speech, you can organize your notes on a timeline, plot diagram, or story board. For example:

1st event	2nd event	3rd event	last event

MODEL SPEECH IN CHRONOLOGICAL ORDER: AN OPENING ANECDOTE

A teacher, a wrestler, and a lawyer wound up together at the Pearly Gates. St. Peter informed them that in order to get into Heaven, they would each have to answer one question.

Addressing the teacher, St. Peter asked, "What was the name of the ship that crashed into the iceberg" The teacher answered quickly, "That would be the Titanic." St. Peter let her through the gate.

Addressing the wrestler, St. Peter asked, "How many people died on the ship?" The wrestler answered, "About 1,500." St. Peter let him through the gate.

St. Peter then turned to the lawyer. "Name them."

DEDUCTIVE AND INDUCTIVE ORGANIZATION

Inductive speeches arrive at general principles from particular facts or instances. This method of organization moves from the specific to the general. It begins with facts and proceeds to a general conclusion.

Deductive speeches are the opposite; the process of reasoning moves from general claims to specific instances. Deductive

ZIP TIPS

To use deductive reasoning correctly, you must first make sure that the major premise is true. If the major premise is flawed, your logic will collapse like Enron.

arguments are called *syllogisms* and have three parts: two premises and a conclusion. The structure (and an example) looks like this:

Major Premise:	All humans are mortal.
Minor Premise:	All Greeks are humans.
Conclusion:	Therefore, all Greeks are mortal.

The following chart summarizes these two classic forms of structuring your speeches.

Inductive	Deductive
Argument begins with specific evidence	Argument begins with a general claim
Argument ends with a general claim	Argument ends with a specific evidence

Inductive reasoning and deductive reasoning are the basis of many classic persuasive speeches.

MODEL SPEECH IN DEDUCTIVE ORDER: DECLARATION OF INDEPENDENCE

The *Declaration of Independence* is the classic deductive argument. This written manifesto would have been delivered as a speech . . . had not King George ordered all rebels hanged. Here is the structure.

Major Premise:	When government deliberately seeks to reduce the people under absolute despotism, the people have a right, indeed a

duty, to alter or abolish that form of government and create new guards for their future security.

Minor Premise: The government of Great Britain has deliberately sought to reduce the American people under absolute despotism.

Conclusion: Therefore, the American people have a right, indeed a duty, to abolish their present form of government and create new guards for their future security.

Trace the organization in this excerpt.

. . . We hold these truths to be self-evident, that all men are created equal, that they are endowed by their Creator with certain unalienable Rights, that among these are Life, Liberty, and the pursuit of Happiness.—That to secure these rights, Governments are instituted among Men, deriving their just powers from the consent of the governed,—That whenever any Form of Government becomes destructive of these ends, it is the Right of the People to alter or to abolish it, and to institute new Government, laying its foundation on such principles and organizing its powers in such form, as to them shall seem most likely to effect their Safety and Happiness. Prudence, indeed, will dictate that Governments long established should not be changed for light and transient causes; and accordingly all experience hath shown that mankind are more disposed to suffer, while evils are sufferable than to right themselves by abolishing the forms to which they are accustomed.

But when a long train of abuses and usurpations, pursuing invariably the same Object evinces a design to reduce them under absolute Despotism, it is their right, it is their duty, to throw off such Government, and to provide new Guards for their future security.—Such has been the patient sufferance of these Colonies; and such is now the necessity which constrains them to alter their former Systems of Government. The history of the present King of Great Britain is a history of repeated injuries and usurpations, all having in direct object the establishment of an absolute Tyranny over these States. To prove this, let Facts be submitted to a candid world. He has refused his Assent to Laws, the most wholesome and necessary for the public good. He has forbidden his Governors to pass Laws of immediate and pressing importance, unless suspended in their operation till his Assent should be obtained; and when so suspended, he has utterly neglected to attend to them. He has refused to pass other Laws for the accommodation of large districts of people, unless those people would relinquish the right of Representation in the Legislature, a right inestimable to them and formidable to tyrants only. He has called together legislative bodies at places unusual, uncomfortable, and distant from the depository of their Public Records, for the sole purpose of fatiguing them into compliance with his measures. He has dissolved Representative Houses repeatedly, for opposing with manly firmness his invasions on the rights of the people . . .

PROBLEM-SOLUTION ORDER

Here, you present an issue of pressing concern to your audience and then propose one or more ways to resolve it. This method of organization is especially well-suited to persuasive essays, although it can be used with equal success for informative and entertaining speeches.

You can have multiple solutions, of course. These are usually arranged in climactic order, building from least-to-most effective.

MODEL SPEECH IN PROBLEM-SOLUTION ORDER: MARK TWAIN

Twain addressed the problem of alleged police brutality. Notice the problem-solution organization.

Let us abolish policemen who carry clubs and revolvers, and put in a squad of poets armed to the teeth with poems on Spring and Love. I would be very glad to serve as commissioner, not because I think I am especially qualified, but because I am too tired to work

ZIP TIPS

Be careful who you bash in your jokes. Always consider your audience and never whack people based on their race, disability, or religion. When in doubt, leave the joke out of your speech.

and would like to take a rest. Howells would go well as my deputy. He is tired too, and needs a rest badly.

I would start in at once to elevate, purify, and depopulate the red-light district. I would assign the most soulful poets to that district, all heavily armed with their poems. Take Chauncey Depew as a sample. I would station them on the corners after they had

MORE TO UNZIP

Plato once used a syllogism to describe man as a "featherless biped." When fellow philosopher Diogenes heard Plato's flawed syllogism, he gleefully presented him with a plucked chicken.

rounded up all the depraved people of the district so they could not escape, and then have them read from their poems to the poor unfortunates. The plan would be very effective in causing an emigration of the depraved element.

MORE TO UNZIP

William Dean Howells (1837–1920) was an influential critic, editor, and author. A close friend of Twain's, Howells also helped champion many other now-classic American writers, including Stephen Crane, Emily Dickinson, and Sarah Orne Jewett.

OTHER METHODS OF ORGANIZING YOUR SPEECH

As mentioned in the beginning of this chapter, you've got many choices when it comes to organizing your speeches. Here are some additional methods.

Method	Definition	Most Suitable for Speeches That . . .
Analysis and classification	*Analyze* to divide things into categories; *classify* to group things together	Inform
Comparison and contrast	*Compare* to show how things are similar; *contrast* to show how they are different	Inform, persuade, entertain
Definition	Explain the meaning of a word or concept	Inform and/or entertain
Example	Use specific facts and details	Inform and/or persuade
Spatial	Arrange information by the order of space	Inform and/or entertain
Topical	Arrange ideas by topics	Inform and/or entertain

MODEL SPEECH IN EXAMPLE ORDER: MARK TWAIN

To raise money for a local charity, Twain read one of his stories and described how he had been mocked by an arrogant audience in Vienna, March 10, 1899.

I have not sufficiently mastered German, to allow my using it with impunity. My collection of fourteen-syllable German words is still incomplete. But I have just added to that collection a jewel—a veritable jewel. I found it in a telegram from Linz, and it contains ninety-five letters:

Personaleinkommensteuerschatzungskommissionsmitgliedsreisekostenrechnungsergänzungsrevisionsfund

If I could get a similar word engraved upon my tombstone I should sleep beneath it in peace.

BE GENUINE, BE BRIEF, BE SEATED

Regardless of the method you choose to organize your speech, keep it short and sweet. The average audience can sit for about 20

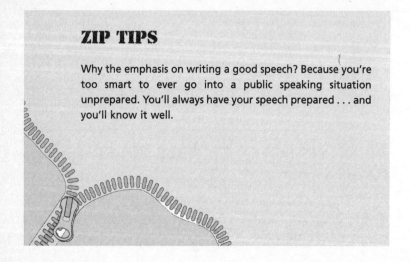

ZIP TIPS

Why the emphasis on writing a good speech? Because you're too smart to ever go into a public speaking situation unprepared. You'll always have your speech prepared . . . and you'll know it well.

minutes without surreptitiously playing video poker on their cell phones. Allocate those 20 minutes as follows:

Amount of Time	Task
1 minute	Introduce yourself, thank the host
2 minutes	Grab the audience with a story, videotape, joke, quotation
15 minutes	Body of your speech
2 minutes	Summary, reiterate your main point

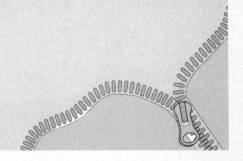

ZIP TIPS

Class lectures, training speeches, and so on will be longer than 20 minutes, of course.

CHAPTER 5

Write This Way

OW OFTEN HAVE you listened to an especially gifted public speaker and said, "Wow! That speaker really touched my soul/set my heart aflutter/taught me something valuable/kept me awake for an entire 20 minutes?" It's not magic . . . nor is it brilliance. It's simply sustained effort. As Michelangelo—no stranger to genius or effort—said as he gazed at the Sistine Chapel's ceiling: *If you knew how much work went into it, you wouldn't call it genius.*

Now that you've learned different ways to organize your ideas, it's time to get your speech down on paper. So fire up your laptop and plant your elbows on the desk. You're going to write a speech.

ERECT THE SCAFFOLD: YOUR OUTLINE

Making an outline before you write your speech forces you to arrange your ideas in a logical sequence. More so, outlines show you the entire structure of your speech at a glance, so you can easily make adjustments before you actually write your speech. Outlines DO follow a set format, so . . .

Format the Outline

Outlines can use Roman numerals or decimals. The choice is yours—as long as you stick with the same format. Your outline can't be half Roman numerals and half decimals—it ends up looking like Michael Jackson (and we don't want *that*.) The following chart shows how to arrange letters and numbers on your outlines.

Outlines can be written in four different formats:

1. Word Outlines
   Each entry is a single word or topic. There's no end punctuation.

2. Phrase Outlines
   Each entry is a phrase. There's no end punctuation.

3. Sentence Outlines
   Each entry is a sentence. There is end punctuation.

4. Paragraph Outlines
   Each entry is a paragraph. There is end punctuation.

As with Roman numerals and decimals, you can't have it all here, either—choose one format and stick with it. Word or phrase outlines are best suited for the early plan-

Division	Roman Numerals	Decimals
Main ideas	Roman numerals: I, II, III, etc.	1.0, 2.0, 3.0, etc.
Subtopics	Capital letters: A, B, C, etc.	1.1, 1.2, 1.3, etc.
Examples	Arabic numbers: 1, 2, 3, etc.	1.2.1, 1.2.2, 1.2.3, etc.
Details	Lower-case letters: a, b, c, etc.	1.2.2.1, 1.2.2.2, 1.2.2.3, etc.

ning phases. These are also much faster and easier to write than a sentence or paragraph outline.

A sentence or paragraph outline provides you with a lot more detail, however. Sentence or paragraph outlines are very effective in the final drafting stages because each helps you write your final speech much more quickly. After all, once you've created a paragraph outline, you've already done all the heavy lifting.

Follow the Rules

Everything has rules, and outlines are no exception. Unlike those arbitrary fashion rules—*Never wear white shoes after Labor Day*—outline rules actually make sense. And here they are.

Entries must come in pairs

You can't have a Roman numeral I without a Roman numeral II; you can't have an A without a B, etc. You can have as many entries as you wish, but you must have at least two of each type.

Entries must be in the same format

As you read earlier, don't mix entry formats. No single-word entries and phrase entries together, for instance.

Entries should be parallel

Parallel structure means that all words, phrases, and sentences have the same grammatical structure. For example: *raising funds, mailing flyers, collecting checks, registering attendees.*

Entries must be subordinated

Subordination means items placed under each other in the outline must be actual subdivisions. Organize your ideas from general to specific or abstract to concrete. Each entry must be directly linked to the entry under which it appears.

Faulty Subordination

    I. Advice for graduates.

        A. Advice for seniors.

        B. Wear sunscreen.

        C. Floss often.

Correct Subordination

    I. Advice for graduates.

        A. Wear sunscreen.

        B. Enjoy your youth.

        C. Floss often.

    II. Advice for seniors

Indent lines to show the relationship of ideas

Main ideas are flush left. Subheads are indented five spaces, examples are five spaces from that, and details are five spaces from that. Below is a sample format. The specific format of your outline will vary, of course, depending on the number of entries you have.

   I. Main idea

      A. Subtopic

      B. Subtopic

  II. Main idea

      A. Subtopic

      B. Subtopic

      C. Subtopic

 III. Main idea

      A. Subtopic
         1. Example
         2. Example

      B. Subtopic

 IV. Main idea

      A. Subtopic

      B. Subtopic
         1. Example
         2. Example

   C. Subtopic
    1. Example
    2. Example
     a. Detail
     b. Detail
     c. Detail

WRITE YOUR OUTLINE

1. First, jot down your topic, purpose, and audience. Here's a model.

   Topic: Advice to newly graduated college students

   Purpose: To entertain

   Audience: College graduates; their parents, relatives, and friends; college faculty, staff, and administration

ZIP TIPS

Recycle. When you're writing your speech, never discard even a single scrap of writing. Just because you can't use what you've just written now doesn't mean that you can't use it in a future speech.

2. Choose an outline form. Write your main ideas first.

3. Add the specific points, details, and examples.

4. Revise your outline. Add missing information. Rearrange information for logic and cohesion.

WRITE YOUR SPEECH

Mark Twain said: *A man who carries a cat by the tail learns something he can learn in no other way.* And so it is with writing a speech. You can't win it if you're not in it, so once you've finished reading this chapter, settle in for the night and write a speech. If you don't have to deliver it tomorrow, write something you anticipate having to deliver (A wedding toast? A job interview speech?) and set it aside for the day when you'll be in the limelight.

Establish a Style

Choose words that help you convey your ideas and suit your purpose and audience. Your speeches will either be formal or informal. The following chart shows this difference.

Type of Speech	Characteristics	Examples
Formal	Long and complex words, intricate figures of speech, few or no contractions, long and complex sentences, little or no humor	Eulogies and commencement addresses
Informal	Everyday words, standard vocabulary, contractions, short sentences, humor	Toasts and roasts

WORDS UNZIPPED

Unity and Cohesion: One idea follows the previous one in a logical way. You can add *transitions* (linking words and phrases such as *first*, *second*, *third*) to help create unity, but the basic arrangement of your ideas must still follow a clear method of organization.

MODEL SPEECH: SUSAN B. ANTHONY

In the 1800s, women in the U.S. had few legal rights—not even the right to vote. Famous suffragette Susan B. Anthony gave the following speech after her arrest for casting an illegal vote in the presidential election of 1872. She was tried and then fined $100, but refused to pay. Decide whether the style of her speech is formal or informal.

Friends and fellow citizens: I stand before you tonight under indictment for the alleged crime of having voted at the last presidential election, without having a lawful right to vote. It shall be my work this evening to prove to you that in thus voting, I not only committed no crime, but, instead, simply exercised my citizen's rights, guaranteed to me and all United States citizens by the National Constitution, beyond the power of any state to deny.

The preamble of the Federal Constitution says: "We, the people of the United States, in order to form a more perfect union, establish justice, insure domestic tranquility, provide for the common defense, promote the general welfare, and secure the blessings of liberty to ourselves and our posterity, do ordain and establish this Constitution for the United States of America."

It was we, the people; not we, the white male citizens; nor yet we, the male citizens; but we, the whole people, who formed the Union. And we formed it, not to give the blessings of liberty, but to secure them; not to the half of ourselves and the half of our posterity, but to the whole people—women as well as men.

And it is a downright mockery to talk to women of their enjoyment of the blessings of liberty while they are denied the use of the only means of securing them provided by this democratic-republican government—the ballot.

For any state to make sex a qualification that must ever result in the disfranchisement of one entire half of the people, is to pass a bill of attainder, or, an ex post facto law, and is therefore a violation of the supreme law of the land. By it the blessings of liberty are forever withheld from women and their female posterity.

To them this government has no just powers derived from the consent of the governed. To them this government is not a democracy. It is not a republic. It is an odious aristocracy; a hateful oligarchy of sex; the most hateful aristocracy ever established on the face of the globe; an oligarchy of wealth, where the rich govern the poor. An oligarchy of learning, where the educated govern the ignorant, or even an oligarchy of race, where the Saxon rules the African, might be endured; but this oligarchy of sex, which makes *father, brothers, husband, sons, the oligarchs over the mother and sisters, the wife and daughters, of every household—which ordains all men sovereigns, all women subjects, carries dissension, discord, and rebellion into every home of the nation.*

Webster, Worcester, and Bouvier all define a citizen to be a person in the United States, entitled to vote and hold office.

The only question left to be settled now is: Are women persons? And I hardly believe any of our opponents will have the hardihood to say they are not. Being persons, then, women are citizens; and no state has a right to make any law, or to enforce any old law, that shall abridge their privileges or immunities. Hence, every discrimination against women in the constitutions and laws of the several states is today null and void, precisely as is every one against Negroes.

As you craft your style, consider these elements as well:

- Clichés.
  Clichés are stale expressions, such as *the wind beneath my wings, lo and behold, lie like a rug, gentle as a lamb.* As a general rule, avoid clichés because they're meaningless. They make your speech hackneyed and even corny.

- Euphemisms.
  Euphemisms are a nice way of saying something that might offend your audience. For instance, rather than saying, "Your gerbil died," you might say, "You gerbil

passed on," or "Your gerbil has gone to its final reward." While euphemisms are often necessary for social tact (you would say, "Your son is working below his potential" rather than "Little Billy is a moron"), using the correct term helps ensure that your audience will understand you.

- Offensive language.
  There's a lot of this: sexist language (*girl* for *woman*); racist language; socially taboo language, such as curses; ageist terms (*geezer* for *mature person*); and terms that discriminate against the handicapped. It goes without saying that you'll never use any offensive language in any of your speeches.

- Slang and regionalisms.
  Slang is language that passes in and out of use quickly, such as *groovy, my bad*, and *cool*. *Regionalisms* are words used in specific parts of the country, such as *pop* or *soda* for carbonated beverages. Avoid regionalisms because they're apt to be misunderstood or not understood at all.

- Rhythm.
  All speech has *rhythm,* its beat. Make your speeches flow rhythmically by using *alliteration, parallelism,* and *repetition.*

MODEL SPEECH: ABRAHAM LINCOLN

See how Lincoln, a master speech writer, created rhythm in the following speech he delivered to group of students in Springfield, Illinois, in 1837.

Here, then, is one point at which danger may be expected. The question recurs, how shall we fortify against it? The answer is simple. Let every American, every lover of liberty, every well-wisher to his posterity, swear by the blood of the Revolution never to violate in the least particular the laws of the country, and never to tolerate their violation by others. As the patriots of seventy-six did to the support of the Declaration of Independence, so to the support of the Constitution and the Law let every American pledge his life, his property, and his sacred honor; let every man remember that to violate the law is to trample on the blood of his father, and to tear the charter of his own and his

ZIP TIPS

As more than one politician has discovered to his or her chagrin, you never know when the microphone is still on. As a result, even if you don't think you're being overheard, *always* assume that Big Brother is listening, so watch your words.

children's liberty. Let reverence for the laws be breathed by every American mother to the lisping babe that prattles on her lap. Let it be taught in schools, in seminaries, and in colleges. Let it be written in primers, spelling-books, and in almanacs. Let it be preached from the pulpit, proclaimed in legislative halls, and enforced in courts of justice. And, in short, let it become the political religion of the nation.

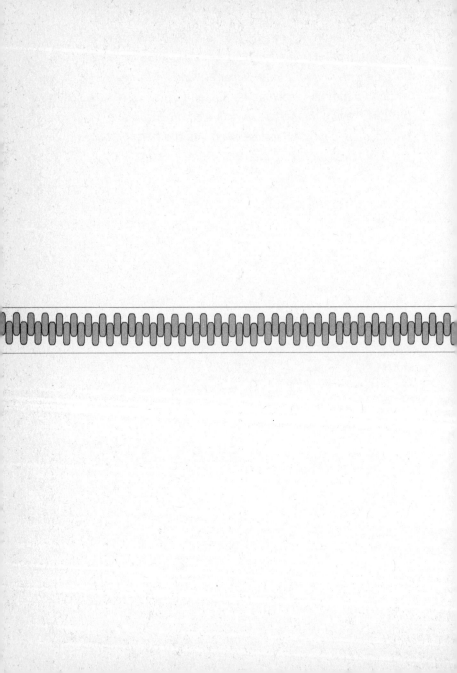

CHAPTER 6

Picture Perfect

WHAT MESSAGE DOES this picture send?

It's your lucky night.

And this picture?

We're in the money, we're in the money.

We all get the message. A well-chosen visual telegraphs your main idea, communicates your message clearly, and saves you time when you speak. In addition, a well-designed visual can often communicate information that's difficult to put into words.

So far, you've learned the importance of crafting a solid speech. You've learned to speak logically on a topic that appeals to your audience. How can you make your speech even more effective? Add visuals.

WORDS UNZIPPED

Visuals: Any picture, including PowerPoint, photographs, maps, charts, pictures, films, displays, models, blackboards and chalk, and so on.

GUIDELINES FOR USING VISUALS

A Harvard University study revealed that people understand and remember only 7 percent of the information delivered solely by speech. In contrast, people remember 87 percent of information delivered both verbally and visually. What does this mean for you? If you want people to forget your message, avoid visuals. But if you'd prefer to make a lasting impression, persuade your audience, and convey information, present your message with both words and visuals. Let's look at how to get the most bang for your visual aid buck.

Learn About the Different Visual Aids Available

The range is nearly limitless, including posters, overheads, videos, exhibits, 35 mm slides, and computer graphics programs. Become familiar with *all* of these methods so you can pick and choose freely. Also, practice with them when you're not crushed for time. See which ones you feel most comfortable using.

Choose and Design All Visuals Carefully

Suit your visual to your audience, purpose, and speech. Also make sure your visuals won't offend anyone and don't violate copyright laws or disclose confidential information. Show only top-quality videotapes, never those that have been copied over and over. Design professional-looking visuals. Don't use silly smiley faces like this: ☺. In addition, avoid elements that have no place on the visual.

Make Sure You Really Need the Visual

More is not better; it is simply more. Be very certain that each visual serves a specific purpose and you're not just using it to fill time or impress your audience with your skill. And stop playing with the laser pointer already.

K.I.S.S.

Remember the old adage: K.I.S.S. = Keep it Simple (we'll let you figure out what the last "S" stands for . . .).

When you're designing charts, graphs, posters, PowerPoint slides, and other visuals, less information on the graphic is invariably better. Simple graphics give your visuals more punch and make them easier to understand. Cluttered visuals overwhelm your audience because they're difficult to read.

Use one font throughout the entire presentation. Changing fonts midstream is distracting. Also choose a professional font, such as Times New Roman or Veranda.

Be Brief

Unless you're teaching an art appreciation class, your audience won't enjoy staring at your bar graph for half an hour. As a rough rule of thumb, figure that you should display each visual for about 10 seconds. People have short attentions spans, and even the most visually-arresting slides (hot bodies cavorting on the beach during spring break) pale after repeated exposure.

Be Bold

Prepare your visuals so that *everyone* in your audience can see them clearly. There are few things worse than having to say during a speech, "Well, you folks in the back of the room won't be able to see this slide/poster/photograph, so I'll explain what you're missing." How tacky is that?

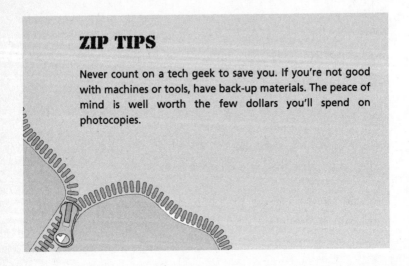

ZIP TIPS

Never count on a tech geek to save you. If you're not good with machines or tools, have back-up materials. The peace of mind is well worth the few dollars you'll spend on photocopies.

Follow the 8H rule: If you can read an image from a distance of eight times its height, the chances are good that your audience will be able to read it when you display it.

Check and Double-Check the Room's Set-Up

Make sure that the room has the technology you need to display your visuals. No offense to anyone, but just because you're promised the sun, moon, and stars doesn't mean you won't arrive in the room to find that the podium has been stolen, the screen won't lower, and the copier is out of toner.

To make sure that your speech goes smoothly, arrive with plenty of spare time so you can personally check that the electrical outlets work, everything interfaces nicely, and so on. Review any videotapes ahead of time to make sure their sound and visual quality are good from beginning to end, too.

Bring Everything You Need

Don't expect extension cords, photocopying facilities, spare laptops, and so on, to be there for you—even if you are told otherwise. People make mistakes. Bring your laptop. Bring sufficient numbers of all handouts. Bring plug adapters. Imagine that you're going to the North Pole with Harold and Kumar. Bring your own seal meat and snowshoes.

Don't Be Upstaged by Your Visuals

Experienced actors try to avoid performing with kids and animals because they (rightly) fear being upstaged by some adorable drooling toddler or a precious little Teacup ShitzapooSpanaDoo. Computer-based presentations allow you to create some really impressive visuals, but you don't want them to be so impressive that everyone ignores what you're saying to concentrate on the pictures and special effects.

Is that Po-TAY-To or Po-TAT-To?

It may sound silly, but make sure you can correctly pronounce all the words on your visuals. Most students have a good reading vocabulary, but likely have not heard many of the words they've read pronounced out loud. So check the pronunciation of all the words you want to use. And if you're not sure how a word is said, don't use the word. Find a good synonym. Also remember that some words are pronounced differently in different parts of the country. Be especially aware of this if you attend a school far away from your hometown.

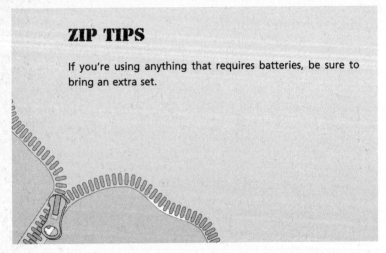

ZIP TIPS

If you're using anything that requires batteries, be sure to bring an extra set.

HIGH-TECH AUDIO/VISUAL AIDS

In addition to formatting your outlines, you can use a software program to create them. These programs have become increasingly popular; indeed, some professional organizations demand that their speakers use them. The best-known is PowerPoint from Microsoft®. As with the other programs, PowerPoint provides the ability to create output for overheads, handouts, speaker notes, and film recorders.

Here's a sample PowerPoint slide:

TEAM PROJECT REQUIREMENTS

Working in a three-person team, you will produce a report of substance, scope, and complexity. The report will have three parts: a research section that includes an overview of laws/legislation and how it applies to the topic; a first-hand observation report of the situation; and evaluations and recommendations.

- **Oral Reports:** At stated times, teams will give oral progress presentation, each team member participating.

- **In-class assignments:** You will be required to write memos, letters, and progress reports in class.

- **Web page:** Each team will create its own Web page and update it at least twice a month.

Follow these guidelines when using this kind of computer software.

- Less is still more.
    Consider the slides as a word/topic outline, so put

relatively little on each slide. Each slide should contain only your key speaking points.

- Use colors judiciously to enhance your message.
Select one color pallet and stick to it. Too many colors are distracting and tend to obscure your message.

- Don't overdo the special effects.
Just because you have access to all the special effects doesn't mean you have to use them. The whoosh sounds, pixilating slides, and swirling visuals are distracting. They can even be unintentionally amusing, as bored people in the audience often echo the sounds to heckle the speaker. Even though it *is* a lot of fun to say *whoosh!* each time a new slide pops up, choose only the ones that help you convey your message.

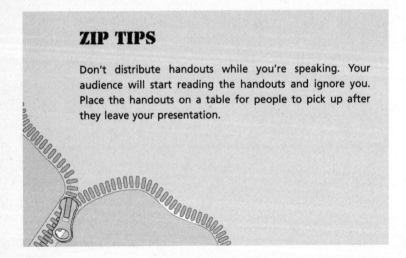

ZIP TIPS

Don't distribute handouts while you're speaking. Your audience will start reading the handouts and ignore you. Place the handouts on a table for people to pick up after they leave your presentation.

LOW-TECH AUDIO/VISUAL AIDS

Don't discard the traditional visual aids just because we now have all these impressive technological bells and whistles. For example, blackboards and flipcharts are both easy to use and easy to see. They also keep your hands busy, which can reduce nervousness. If you do decide to use these visuals, don't turn your back to your audience as you draw and write. Also be very sure you know how to spell all the words you're using.

Posters are also very effective visuals. They're inexpensive and relatively easy to make. You can also have professional printers create enlargements of photographs and charts to use as posters. Use a wooden or laser pointer to call out key points. And remember, make sure that everyone can see every part of your poster. Otherwise, it will harm your speech rather than help it.

Last but not least, experiment with visuals and technology. The type of visual you use is limited only by your imagination and the technology available to you. Have fun with visuals; your audience will appreciate your enthusiasm.

CHAPTER 7

Yes, You Can Sound
Like That!

WILLIAM SHAKESPEARE WAS an actor as well as a playwright, so he didn't hesitate to give his actors directions while performing his plays. A public speech is a performance just like any acting gig. As a result, Hamlet's famous advice in the play of the same name holds true for public speakers as well:

Speak the speech, I pray you, as I pronounced it to you, trippingly on the tongue. But if you mouth it, as many of our players do, I had as lief [willingly] the town crier spoke my lines. Nor do not saw the air too much with your hand, thus, but use all gently . . . O, it offends me to the soul to hear a robustious periwig-pated [toupee] fellow tear a passion to tatters, to very rags, to split the ears of the groundlings, who for the most part are capable of nothing but inexplicable dumb shows and noise . . .

Sadly, we can't all sound sexy and smoky like Scarlett Johansson and Angelina Jolie. Neither can we all sound scary like James Earl Jones/Darth Vader or creepy like Christopher Walken. Fortunately, however, we all *can* make the most of the voice we have. In this chapter, you'll learn how to improve your vocal quality so you can deliver all your speeches "trippingly on the tongue."

ARTICULATION AND CLARITY

You use your tongue, lips, and other speech organs to make sounds. When you pronounce words correctly, they're clear and

easy to understand. That's because you're articulating carefully and correctly. The best way to check your articulation and clarity is to record your speech. Play back the recording, listening carefully for unclear words. Here are some things to watch for and correct during your practice sessions:

- Placing the emphasis on the wrong syllable.
  If you're not sure how to pronounce a word, try not to use it in your speech. Why make life difficult? If you must use the word, check the dictionary for the correct pronunciation and then practice saying the word until you have it down cold.

- Switching letters.
  Children are famous for this, as in the many ways they mispronounce *hospital*. This can happen more easily to public speakers when they're nervous, so be on your guard.

- Adding letters.
  People often add letters where they don't belong. For example, *jewelry* becomes *jewelery*; *remembrance* becomes *rememberance*. No extra letters, please.

- Dropping letters or sounds.
  Some speakers drop the last letters, such as the "g" in *going*. Say every letter that's supposed to be said.

- Slurring sounds.
  This is one of the most common articulation errors. Speakers slur over some sounds, making the words difficult to understand. Pronounce each word slowly and carefully, like it counts—because it does.

- Having an accent.
  Accents can be charming, but they can also be distracting. If you have an accent, never apologize. Instead, make a special effort to pronounce all words clearly.

PACE

Your *pace* is the rate at which you speak. By varying your pace, you create meaning and audience interest in your speech. Follow these guidelines.

Slow Down!	Speed Up!
Crucial points	Less important points
Complex points	Humorous sections
Serious ideas	Exciting parts

In part, pacing is a regional issue—people in the Northeast tend to speak much more quickly than those in the South, for instance. But nearly all public speakers increase their rate of speech when they're tense. It's that unconscious voice speaking from the dark recesses of your mind: "Get this speech over with as fast as possible!"

Time yourself speaking for one minute. You should be speaking at about 150 words per minute. Adjust your rate until you achieve this pace. Make sure you're not racing to try to hustle off the stage ASAP.

SPEECH IMPEDIMENTS

Speech impediments don't have to be a deterrent to success. Look how far the stutterers Moses, Aesop, Claudius, Aristotle, Isaac Newton, Lewis Carroll, and Winston Churchill got. The same is

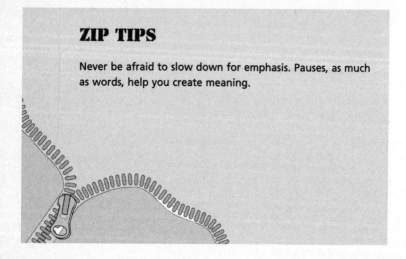

ZIP TIPS

Never be afraid to slow down for emphasis. Pauses, as much as words, help you create meaning.

true today—actors Bruce Willis and James Earl Jones stutter, as does the singer Carly Simon and the TV reporter John Stossel.

So save your worry for things that really matter, like the soaring price of gas, global warming, and *American Idol* hijinks.

MORE TO UNZIPP

Take this quick quiz to see if you can pronounce the following common words correctly. Check your answers in a dictionary.

nuclear	Amish	colonel	chamois	Wednesday
yacht	brooch	draught	suite	hiccough

VOICE QUALITY

Your voice can command the right kind of attention—like an Ivy League diploma on the wall or a private jet in the garage—or the wrong kind of attention—like white stretch pants on a tush the size of a truck. First and foremost, your voice must be easy to understand and flexible. You must be able to vary your rate, pitch,

MORE TO UNZIP

Under the pen name "Lewis Carroll," Charles Lutwidge Dodgson wrote *Alice in Wonderland*. He hoped to become a priest but, according to some accounts, failed to take vows because of his stuttering. Here's part of a poem he wrote.

Learn well your grammar,
And never stammer,
Write well and neatly,
And sing soft sweetly,
Drink tea, not coffee;
Never eat toffy.
Eat bread with butter.
Once more don't stutter.

and force. But if you find that you sound nasal, whiny, or like you've been sucking the air out of a balloon, it's time to work on your voice quality.

You can practice on your own with your trusty tape recorder or you can invest some bucks on a speech therapist. It's probably not a great idea to spend your trust fund on a vocal coach unless you intend to become the next Meryl Streep. But if your voice really bothers you, consider putting in some serious time improving its quality.

VOLUME

Your speech is useless if no one can hear you. Or if only the people in the "expensive seats" can hear you. You must have sufficient volume. The *volume* is the loudness at which you speak.

The further away your audience is, the louder you must speak. The problem is that your voice always seems so loud when you're standing at the front of the room, you're afraid you're shouting. How can you figure out if you can be heard?

WORDS UNZIPPED

Pitch: The depth of a tone or sound. Pitch depends on how fast your vocal cords vibrate. Speak in your normal pitch, but be aware that your pitch will usually be higher if you're nervous. Tape yourself to see if you're getting squeaky.

- Before the speech, do a test run in the room. Place a few volunteers in the very back to see if they can hear you.

- Determine if you need amplification. If so, get a microphone and use it.

PRACTICE SPEECH

King Edward VIII (1894–1972) was a British dolt, but his following speech has become a classic. Edward became the King of England after the death of his father, George V, on January 20, 1936. Edward had fallen for Wallis Warfield Simpson, an American dolt. Mummy and Daddy didn't approve of Wallis—not because she was as dumb as a piece of toast. No, it was because she was an American and had been married twice (her second divorce was still pending). On December 10, 1936, King Edward submitted his abdication to marry Wallis.

Use this as a practice speech.

At long last I am able to say a few words of my own. I have never wanted to withhold anything, but until now it has not been constitutionally possible for me to speak.

A few hours ago I discharged my last duty as King and Emperor, and now that I have been succeeded by my brother, the Duke of York, my first words must be to declare my allegiance to him. This I do with all my heart.

You all know the reasons which have impelled me to renounce the throne. But I want you to understand that in making up my mind I did not forget the country or the empire, which, as Prince of Wales and lately as King, I have for twenty-five years tried to serve.

But you must believe me when I tell you that I have found it impossible to carry the heavy burden of responsibility and to discharge my duties as King as I would wish to do without the help and support of the woman I love.

And I want you to know that the decision I have made has been mine and mine alone. This was a thing I had to judge entirely for myself. The other person most nearly concerned has tried up to the last to persuade me to take a different course.

I have made this, the most serious decision of my life, only upon the single thought of what would, in the end, be best for all. This decision has been made less difficult to me by the sure knowledge that my brother, with his long training in the public affairs of this country and with his fine qualities, will be able to take my place forthwith without interruption or injury to the life and progress of the empire. And he has one matchless blessing, enjoyed by so many of you, and not bestowed on me—a happy home with his wife and children.

During these hard days I have been comforted by her majesty my mother and by my family. The ministers of the crown, and in particular, Mr. Baldwin, the Prime Minister, have always treated me with full consideration. There has never been any constitutional difference between me and them, and between me and Parliament. Bred in the constitutional tradition by my father, I should never have allowed any such issue to arise.

Ever since I was Prince of Wales, and later on when I occupied the throne, I have been treated with the greatest kindness by all classes of the people wherever I have lived or journeyed throughout the empire. For that I am very grateful.

I now quit altogether public affairs and I lay down my burden. It may be some time before I return to my native land, but I shall always follow the fortunes of the British race and empire with profound interest, and if at any time in the future I can be found of service to his majesty in a private station, I shall not fail.

And now, we all have a new King. I wish him and you, his people, happiness and prosperity with all my heart. God bless you all! God save the King!

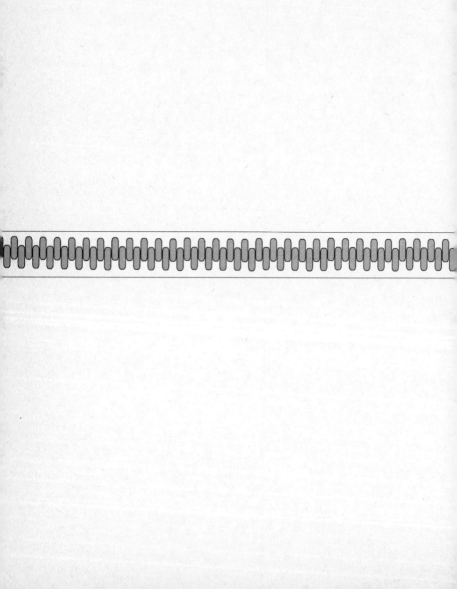

CHAPTER 8

Hot Bodies

CONSIDER THIS SITUATION: You walk into a bar and sit down next to a cute stud muffin. As you admire his goodies, you smile. He crosses his arms across his chest, tosses his head back, sneers, and turns away.

Consider this situation: You walk into a bar and sit down next to a cute stud muffin. As you admire his goodies, you smile. He places his arms on his knees, looks into your eyes, smiles, and leans toward you.

Not a word has been spoken, but you've gotten the message loud and clear. In the first situation, it's just not happening. In the second situation, it's going to be an interesting night.

How is it possible to communicate without language? It's more than possible; it's the way we send a significant portion of our messages.

WHO NEEDS WORDS?

Your body reveals a lot about your mood, attitude, and emotions. In fact, according to scholars of this sort of thing, *more than half* of what we "say" is communicated nonverbally, through our body language. Communicating through body language is vital in daily situations, especially when it comes to public speaking. Of course we still need words, but without the appropriate accompanying gestures, we're sending mixed messages—at best. At worst, we've got a total failure to communicate.

As a public speaker, strong body language is the decisive way that you:

- Build credibility.

- Convey your meaning.

- Express your feelings.

- Connect with your audience.

DO THE MATH

To be an effective public speaker, you must learn how to match your nonverbal and verbal communication, your gestures and words. One reinforces the other, like Shakira's voice and her hips.

Here's the equation:

$$
\begin{array}{l}
\text{The Right Words in the Right Places} \\
\underline{+ \text{ The Right Gestures in the Right Places}} \\
= \text{Meaningful Speeches}
\end{array}
$$

What makes effective body language especially challenging is getting your words and gestures in synch. Try taping yourself giving a speech. Then watch it. The odds are good that you'll be shocked to discover that your body language doesn't always match your meaning. For instance, some people shake their head "no" when they say "yes."

Practice matching your gestures to your message. The most powerful speakers use meaningful, recognizable gestures that reinforce their message, mood, and goal. But don't over-analyze body language. Remember that sometimes a cigar is just a cigar . . . not a phallic symbol. As you give your speeches, try to use gestures that feel natural, look natural, and elicit the response you want from your audience.

According to a group of small kids: "The body consists of three parts—the brainium, the borax, and the abominable cavity. The brainium contains the brain, the borax contains the heart and lungs, and the abominable cavity contains the bowels, of which there are five: a, e, i, o, and u." Hmmmm.

Fortunately, bodies—and body language—are a lot simpler. And you probably know a lot more about body

WORDS UNZIPPED

Nonverbal communication: The series of gestures, stances, facial expressions, and movements that we use to communicate meaning.

language than you realize. Let's start with the basics for public speakers—the eyes.

EYE CONTACT

The Elizabethans believed that the eyes were the windows to the soul, and they were clearly on to something. Effective public speakers convey a great deal of meaning through eye contact.

Start by making eye contact with members of the audience. Since a public speech isn't a staring contest over the dinner table, use the 3-second rule: Look straight into the eyes of a person in the audience for 3 seconds at a time. If looking straight into someone's eyes gives you the creeps, look at their forehead. They'll never know the difference, and you won't be as nervous. Intersperse direct eye contact with a general sweep of the audience. How do you know when to make eye contact and when to do the sweep? Match the eye contact to the meaning. For instance, if you're trying to make a sincere point, go with individual eye contact. If your message is broader, use the eye sweep.

One great benefit of eye contact is the feedback it gives you. If people look back at you, you can tell your speech is effective. If they look down, you may be bombing. If that's the case, slow down, take a breath, and use the rest of your body, as well as your eyes, to convey your sincerity.

POSTURE

"Stand up straight!" your mother harassed. "You slump over like Uncle Louie." Mom was on to something. Good posture conveys honesty. After all, an upright speaker must be an upright person. Hey, we didn't say this body language stuff was fair or even logical, just that it's the way our culture works.

Your stance shows if you're confident or scared silly. How you hold yourself indicates whether you're happy or despondent. Walk up to the podium like you own the place. Once there, stand up straight rather than hunching over like you're clutching a life preserver. Point your feet straight ahead, a bit less than shoulder-width apart. Lean forward to make a point or to suggest that you're open to an idea. This works especially well during question-and-answer sessions.

Under no circumstances should you sway back and forth. Your audience will get seasick. It's amazing how many speakers do this . . . and how distracting it is.

HAND GESTURES

Your hands are one of the most effective ways you have of emphasizing a point,

WORDS UNZIPPED

Shill: Someone you plant in the audience to praise and support you out of friendship and loyalty. Put Momma and Poppa in the front row if that will calm you down; leave them home if they'll make you more nervous with their wide grins and enthusiastic applause.

expressing emotion, and engaging your audience. They're also a great way to help you release stress and thus feel less nervous.

You already have a vocabulary of hand gestures all memorized. Eliminate the ones we use while driving and adjust the rest to your audience and purpose. For instance, what works one-on-one often doesn't work when you're speaking before a large audience, simply because you're further from the audience. Follow these guidelines to become a hands-on speaker:

- The smaller the crowd, the smaller and faster your gestures should be.

- The bigger the crowd, the bigger and slower your gestures. Start your gestures from your shoulder rather than your hands to get them large enough to communicate your meaning to a crowd. Also be sure that your gestures can be seen over a podium. Hold your hands high.

- Hold your hands wide open to show that you're sincere.

- Match your gestures to your words. For instance, if you're counting, hold out your fingers and count on them.

- At least some of the time, hold your hands behind your back during question-and-answer sessions. This suggests you're open to new ideas.

- Try to keep your hands out of your pockets, as this suggests you have something to hide.

- Crossed arms indicate defensiveness and the desire to be out of the situation.

- Avoid clenching your fists and placing your hands on your hips. Both gestures suggest aggression.

- Under no circumstances should you cross your hands over your groin. You're not Adam or Eve, and you're sure not in the Garden of Eden. Leave the privates alone.

- Use transitional gestures to indicate that you're moving from one part of the speech to another. For instance, move both hands, palms facing down, from left to right.

- Practice eliminating distracting or nervous gestures, such as playing with your hair.

Also, know when *not* to use your hands. Letting your hands fall to your sides between gestures conveys self-confidence. Standing still serves to reinforce all your gestures by amplifying them through contrast.

PRACTICE SPEECH

Apply what you learned about body language by delivering part of Marc Antony's famous speech about the murder of Julius Caesar. Antony, in danger himself, wants to avenge Caesar's death. Here's how he does it.

Friends, Romans, countrymen, lend me your ears;
I come to bury Caesar, not to praise him.
The evil that men do lives after them;
The good is oft interred with their bones;
So let it be with Caesar. The noble Brutus
Hath told you Caesar was ambitious:
If it were so, it was a grievous fault,
And grievously hath Caesar answer'd it.
Here, under leave of Brutus and the rest—
For Brutus is an honorable man;
So are they all, all honorable men—
Come I to speak in Caesar's funeral.
He was my friend, faithful and just to me:
But Brutus says he was ambitious;

ZIP TIPS

Don't use the same gestures over and over. No matter how effective you think they are, repetitive gestures become meaningless. They eventually become annoying, or even amusing, as audience members mimic the gesture to mock you. Sigh. Audiences can be cruel.

And Brutus is an honorable man.
He hath brought many captives home to Rome
Whose ransoms did the general coffers fill:
Did this in Caesar seem ambitious?
When that the poor have cried, Caesar hath wept:
Ambition should be made of sterner stuff:
Yet Brutus says he was ambitious;

MORE TO UNZIP

Brilliant comedians create their effects in large part through their body language, using their bodies to underscore, or even create, humor. Think about their dumbstruck facial expressions, eloquent shrugs, and little dances.

And Brutus is an honorable man.
You all did see that on the Lupercal
I thrice presented him a kingly crown,
Which he did thrice refuse: was this ambition?
Yet Brutus says he was ambitious;
And, sure, he is an honorable man.
I speak not to disprove what Brutus spoke,
But here I am to speak what I do know.
You all did love him once, not without cause:
What cause withholds you then, to mourn for him?
O judgment! thou art fled to brutish beasts,
And men have lost their reason. Bear with me;
My heart is in the coffin there with Caesar,
And I must pause till it come back to me.

Remember this: Penguins are adorable, but they'd make lousy public speakers. Despite their formal dress, they don't use any body language at all. And what's with those flippers always at their sides? What message does *that* send?

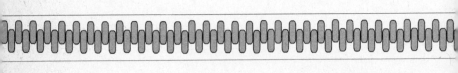

CHAPTER 9

How to Save a Life— Your Own

QUESTION: How do you get to Carnegie Hall?

ANSWER: Practice, practice, practice.

It's an old joke, but it has withstood the test of time because it's true. Practice really *does* make perfect. Practice also reduces jitters, a big consideration if you're prone to stomach-churning, hand-trembling, forehead-dripping stage fright. No matter how often you speak in public, practice will help you get better.

GENERAL GUIDELINES FOR REHEARSING

Speech rehearsal, like exercise, is useless, and even harmful, if done incorrectly.

Rehearsing a speech isn't a one-shot event; rather, it's a process. Start the process by setting aside quiet, quality time to rehearse. Also, be sure to allow sufficient time to complete the process. How much time do you need? You'll need to start a few weeks before your actual speech. The more important the speech, the more time you'll need to prepare.

As you rehearse, try these suggestions.

- Try to create the same atmosphere in which you'll be speaking.

Of course you can't gather 100 strangers to address, and we sure don't want you lining up your stuffed animals or Persian cats to watch you. But you *can* dress as you will for your speech, incorporate all your body language, and rehearse using your visual aids. This will help you make sure that the clothing you've chosen is comfortable, your body language conveys your meaning, and your visual aids are easily manipulated.

- Rehearse your speech standing up.
  But you can leave your iPod and TV on. Having some background noise more accurately mirrors the actual speaking situation you'll face. You'll never be speaking in a vacuum—someone will sneeze, cough, or shuffle in late. A cell phone will always go off.

- Rehearse your speech aloud.
  It goes without saying, but we'll say it anyway—speak slowly and clearly. No mumbling under your breath.

- Mark your script.
  As you rehearse, mark your script to indicate which words get the most emphasis. Mark where you want to slow down and where you want to speed up, too.

- Time your speech.
  Revise your speech to suit the established time limit.

PLAYING WITH YOURSELF

There are many delightful ways to amuse yourself, but the best use of your time when you're about to give a speech is spent rehearsing. If you choose to practice alone, stand in front of a mirror. Watch yourself carefully. See if you're happy with your performance. Time yourself, too, to help track your pacing.

PLAYING WITH OTHERS

Or, you can rehearse your speech in front of one or more people. This helps you practice eye contact and get feedback about your content and delivery. Be careful whom you choose as your audience, however. You don't want someone who will say, "Oooo, baby, you are so hot." While that's good for your self-esteem, you're not concerned with getting all puffed up here. What you want is a person or people who will give you honest feedback. Arm your crowd with paper and pencils and have them complete the following worksheet as you deliver your speech.

ZIP TIPS

What should you do if you make a mistake while you're rehearsing? The first few times, correct it. By your final rehearsal, however, do exactly what you would do during the final speech: Soldier on if the mistake is minor; pause and correct it if it's major.

What was the central message of my speech?	
How well did I communicate it?	
What was my purpose—to persuade, entertain, inform? How do you know?	
Which gestures were especially effective?	
Did I speak at the correct pace—not too fast and not too slow?	1 = needs improvement 2 = adequate 3 = outstanding
Did I pronounce each word correctly?	1 = needs improvement 2 = adequate 3 = outstanding
Was I loud enough to be heard clearly?	1 = needs improvement 2 = adequate 3 = outstanding
Did I avoid unnecessary "fillers" such as *eh, uh*, and *like*?	1 = needs improvement 2 = adequate 3 = outstanding
How well did I handle visual aids?	1 = needs improvement 2 = adequate 3 = outstanding

If this crowd doesn't have any advice to offer or tells you that you're so wonderful and just getting more precious by the minute, get a new crowd.

USING A VIDEO OR TAPE RECORDER

An especially effective rehearsal technique is tape recording or videotaping your speech. This allows you (or someone brutally honest) to review your vocal and physical mannerisms.

As you look at the tape, check that you've made sufficient eye contact. Also make sure that your facial mannerisms and gestures mirror your meaning, reinforcing it rather than undermining it. In addition, be on the lookout for any weird facial twitches and oddball mannerisms, such as sticking your fingers in places they don't belong. These mannerisms have to go. Right now.

ZIP TIPS

If you find during rehearsal that your speech is running long, avoid the temptation to fix the problem by speaking faster. Instead, cut your speech judiciously.

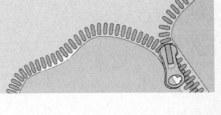

IT'S ALL IN YOUR HEAD

A famous speaker walks into a room, waving his prepared speech. He gazes out at the sea of expectant faces and smiles. Then he raises his papers high and says, "As you can see, I have my speech all prepared, but because of the deep importance of this evening, I feel compelled to speak off-the-cuff, straight from my heart." To everyone's astonishment, he crumbles his speech and throws the papers on the floor.

Then he delivers his precisely prepared speech . . . which he had memorized.

Many speakers have succeeded with this clever gambit and you can, too. Above all else, it proves the importance of being completely, thoroughly, and absolutely prepared.

That said, do you have to memorize your speech? No.

FOUR METHODS FOR DELIVERING YOUR SPEECH

You've got some choices of delivery systems here. Four, to be exact. They are:

1. Impromptu

2. Extemporaneous

3. Full script

4. Memorized

Let's see the advantages and disadvantages of each one.

Impromptu

This is spontaneous, unrehearsed public speaking. Think of this as walking on a high wire without a net. Impromptu speaking does have the advantage of being, well, totally and completely unrehearsed.

MORE TO UNZIP

Winston Churchill was ranked the top speaker in Parliament even though he stuttered. He went to great lengths to overcome his stuttering. First, Churchill wrote out his speeches weeks before he had to deliver them. Then he memorized them. And he practiced over and over.

If you're the kind of person who enjoys playing with Rotweilers or sticking your hands in the lions' cage at the zoo, impromptu speaking is for you. But if you like to be organized, relaxed, and well-prepared, you'll probably want to choose another option.

Extemporaneous

This is speaking from prepared notes, such as an outline, index cards, or PowerPoint slides. This is the type of public speaking that most good teachers, managers, and executives use. Extemporaneous speaking allows you to prepare, rehearse, and include audiovisual aides in your presentation. Since you've got notes in front of you and have rehearsed extensively, you're secure, yet flexible. And because you're not married to a script, you can adjust your presentation based on audience feedback. Rehearsal is essential to make this a success.

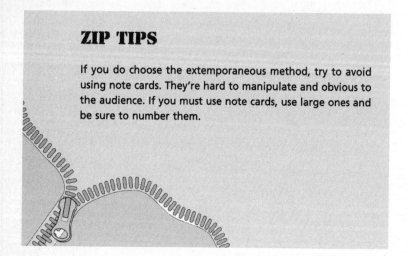

ZIP TIPS

If you do choose the extemporaneous method, try to avoid using note cards. They're hard to manipulate and obvious to the audience. If you must use note cards, use large ones and be sure to number them.

Over time, many extemporaneous speeches become memorized speeches. For example, teachers who deliver the same extemporaneous lecture over and over eventually memorize it. This makes their delivery even more relaxed.

But even if you're only delivering the extemporaneous speech once, you should memorize the first 30 seconds and the last 30 seconds. This allows you to establish a rapport with the audience by making eye contact. It also helps you relax because you've got your opening and closing down pat.

Full Script

In this speaking mode, you've written out the speech. You read it to the audience from a paper copy or a TelePrompTer. Clearly, reading from a script is great because you know exactly what you're going to say, so there's less chance of a blooper. However, listening to someone read a speech is about as exciting as watching grass grow or paint peel. Zzzzzzzzzz. Wake us when it's over.

Memorized

In this situation, you've written and memorized your speech. This allows you control over what you say. At the same time, you can relax and have eye contact with the audience. The big drawback? Memory lapses. If you forget a piece, you can quickly shift into panic mode. Further, it takes a lot of time to memorize a speech. However, if you choose to memorize your speech, keep a copy of the script on the lectern in case you have a brain fart.

There's no saying you can't combine methods to suit your speech to your situation. For instance, you can memorize key sections and speak extemporaneously for the rest of the speech. This gives you the best of both possible worlds.

PRACTICE SPEECH

Yankees first baseman Lou Gehrig, nicknamed "Pride of the Yankees," played in 2,130 consecutive games from 1925 to 1939, setting a major league record. He delivered the following speech, July 4, 1939, in front of 60,000 fans at Yankee Stadium to confirm that he had amyotrophic lateral sclerosis (now often called Lou Gehrig's disease) and was retiring from baseball. He died less than 2 years later. Practice delivering this speech. It's a honey.

Fans, for the past 2 weeks you have been reading about a bad break I got. Yet today I consider myself the luckiest man on the face

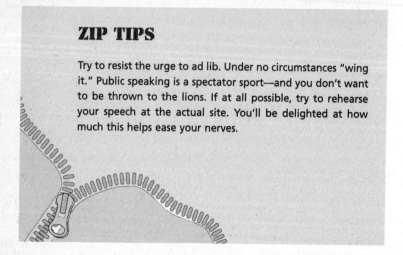

ZIP TIPS

Try to resist the urge to ad lib. Under no circumstances "wing it." Public speaking is a spectator sport—and you don't want to be thrown to the lions. If at all possible, try to rehearse your speech at the actual site. You'll be delighted at how much this helps ease your nerves.

of the earth. I have been in ballparks for 17 years and have never received anything but kindness and encouragement from you fans.

Look at these grand men. Which of you wouldn't consider it the highlight of his career to associate with them for even one day?

Sure, I'm lucky. Who wouldn't consider it an honor to have known Jacob Ruppert—also the builder of baseball's greatest empire, Ed Barrow—to have spent the next 9 years with that wonderful little fellow Miller Huggins—then to have spent the next 9 years with that outstanding leader, that smart student of psychology—the best manager in baseball today, Joe McCarthy!

Sure, I'm lucky. When the New York Giants, a team you would give your right arm to beat, and vice versa, sends you a gift, that's something! When everybody down to the groundskeepers and those boys in white coats remember you with trophies, that's something.

When you have a wonderful mother-in-law who takes sides with you in squabbles against her own daughter, that's something. When you have a father and mother who work all their lives so that you can have an education and build your body, it's a blessing! When you have a wife who has been a tower of strength and shown more courage than you dreamed existed, that's the finest I know.

So I close in saying that I might have had a tough break—but I have an awful lot to live for!

CHAPTER 10
No One Likes the Smelly Kid

If you once forfeit the confidence of your fellow citizens, you can never regain their respect and esteem. You may fool some of the people some of the time, you can even fool some of the people all the time, but you can't fool all the people all of the time.

Abraham Lincoln

All those clichés you grew up hearing are true:

> *First impressions do matter.*

> *You never get a second chance to make a good first impression.*

> *Mother always knows best.*

> *Lightning never strikes in the same place twice.*

OK, maybe not that last one.

Right or wrong, people *do* judge you on your appearance. This may not matter when you're taking out the trash or walking the pooch, but it does matter when you're giving a speech. Especially at the start of your speech, how you look can matter as much (if not more) than what you say. So let's make sure that you're all spiffed up for the big day.

CLEAN UP!

It seems obvious to say this, but judging by the number of people who don't spend sufficient time on personal hygiene—get clean. Really clean. Shower before your speech and take care of all that personal grooming stuff: shaving, shampooing, applying deodorant, nail trimming, tooth brushing, flossing, and rinsing with mouthwash. Never, ever, ever drench yourself in perfume to mask the B.O. You'll stink up the place.

And while we're on the topic of perfume and cologne, how much should you wear when you give a speech? None. That's right—none. Many people are allergic to perfume. And you don't want the audience paying more attention to your patchouli-floral-aroma-with-just-a-hint-of-musk than to your words.

If you smoke, be sure to suck on a breath mint before your speech. This is especially important if you're addressing an intimate audience.

CLOTHING CHOICE

People notice many things about you—some that you can control, some that you can't. For example, you can't do anything about your gender (well, you can, but that's really beyond the scope of this book), but you *can* do a lot about the way you dress.

Best case scenario, about 90 percent of your body is covered by clothing. This is a very good thing because, as Mark Twain said:

Clothes make the man. Naked people have little or no influence on society. Also, clothes are very useful because we don't want to see your naughty bits.

Audiences will judge you on your clothing. Dressing inappropriately or badly—in stained shirts or scuffed shoes—conveys contempt for your audience. That's because clothing is one of the clearest ways that we have to show respect for others. "Judge me on my words and body language, not my clothing," you say. As far as your audience is concerned, clothes help to make you credible. As an overall guideline, dress for a speech as if you were dressing for an important job interview.

ZIP TIPS

Guys, don't button the bottom button of your jacket. It's just not done.

CLOTHING GUIDELINES FOR MALE SPEAKERS

- Wear a suit or its equivalent.
  Why? Because suits and sports jackets indicate power and authority. You're in charge, so you want to look the part.

- Your clothing must fit.
  This is why we have tailors. Pay the money and get your suit tailored so that it fits just right. For instance, about ½" of your shirt cuff must show below your jacket sleeve.

- Never wear a short-sleeved shirt with a tie.
  Short-sleeved shirts scream "low class." They're perfect if you're the manager of a fast-food joint or an off-track betting parlor, but not if you want to project a professional image on the podium.

- Your shoes should be clean and shined.
  They should be appropriate for the occasion—no sneakers or boat shoes for public speeches, please. If you're wearing a suit, wear lace-up shoes.

- Your pants and socks should be on a first-name basis, if not kissing cousins.
  In other words, your pants must be long enough to cover your socks.

- Hide those hairy legs!
  Your socks must cover your shins even when you cross you legs. And they must match your pants.

- Ties should reach your belt line.
  This is neither arbitrary nor negotiable. Too short a tie

makes you look like a hick. And ditch the tie clip or tie tack, unless it represents an organization to which you belong (such as Rotary). In these cases, try to go for a lapel pin instead.

- No pens or pocket protectors in your shirt pocket, please.

  Pens belong inside your suit coat pocket, out of sight. This also applies to Blackberries, cell phones, monster key chains, etc. None of this Superhero utility belt stuff. Store your gear in a good leather briefcase.

- No odd colors or overly trendy styles.

  Go classic—dark blue suit, white shirt, nice solid or subtly patterned tie. No grinning mice, flying geese, or smiley-faces on those ties. If in doubt, go with a solid red tie.

WORDS UNZIPPED

Business casual: Appropriate attire for less-formal speeches. Unfortunately, the term is slippery and doesn't have a clear-cut definition. To most people, *business casual* means pressed khakis and a button-down long-sleeved shirt for men. For women, it's a pair of good pants or a skirt with a formal blouse or twin set.

CLOTHING GUIDELINES FOR FEMALE SPEAKERS

- Despite what you see on television, don't dress in an overly sexy manner.

  The audience shouldn't be treated to a glimpse of your cleavage. Dress as an authoritative, intelligent, competent woman—which is who you are.

- Avoid overly feminine outfits, too.

  Stay away from large floral prints, ruffles, and white peasant blouses. You're not Heidi, yodeling on the mountains.

- So what should you wear?

  Wear a solid color, conservative suit with a matching/coordinated blouse or sweater.

- Your shoes should have no more than 1–2" heel.

  You don't want to be tripping, instead of walking confidently.

- Wear pantyhose. Your feet will thank you for it.

  The pantyhose should be flesh-colored. They can be black if you're wearing a dark dress or suit.

- Unless you're addressing the annual convention of manicurists, no long, elaborate, brightly colored nails, but your nails should be manicured in clear or a light pink.

- Go light on the jewelry.

  As a general rule, put on all your jewelry and then

take off a piece. Avoid any jewelry that you or your audience would find distracting, such as huge dangling chandelier earrings.

- Get a neat, professional hairstyle.
  Make sure your hair isn't obscuring your face.

- Make sure your clothing fits well.
  It should be neither too tight nor too loose.

- When you choose clothing, quality is far more important than trendiness.
  For instance, a good quality leather briefcase will impress your audience more than this year's hot colorful bag.

ZIP TIPS

Don't use the people you see on TV as your guide to good dressing. Instead, consult professional journals or the photos in authoritative newspapers.

FOR THE REST OF YOUR LIFE

Now that you've buffed and shined the outside, it's time to take care of the inside. One of the most important things you can do to ensure that you look your best is to get sufficient sleep the night before. Test yourself with this quick sleeping quiz.

How much sleep does the average adult need to look his or her best, stay healthy, and function at optimal capability? Check one.

[ ] 5–6 hours per night

[ ] 6–7 hours per night

[ ] 8–9 hours per night

It's the last choice: The average adult needs 8–9 hours of sleep every night. "Ha!" you say. "I haven't gotten 8 to 9 hours of sleep a night since I was teething. I'm lucky to get 8 to 9 hours of sleep in two nights." Well, it's time to wake up and go back to sleep. You can teach yourself to sleep less, but you can't teach yourself to need less sleep.

More than 33 percent of people surveyed said they were so sleepy during the day that it interfered with their daily activities. Close to 25 percent said they fell asleep while driving on a regular basis. The National Highway Traffic Safety Administration estimates that drowsy drivers are responsible for 100,000 crashes, 1,500 vehicular deaths, and 71,000 injuries each year.

Take this quick quiz. True or false?

_____ Resting is a good substitute for sleep.

_____ Adults need less sleep as they get older.

_____ You can store up sleep by sleeping more on weekends.

All are false.

MORE TO UNZIP

When all clues to time are removed and people are allowed to sleep as much as they need, they sleep 10.3 hours out of every 24.

START COUNTING SHEEP

If you want to maximize your chances for success on stage, get sufficient sleep. For at least a week before an important speech, try to sleep at least 8 hours every night. Being well-rested raises your self-esteem, increases your ability to focus, and extends your attention span.

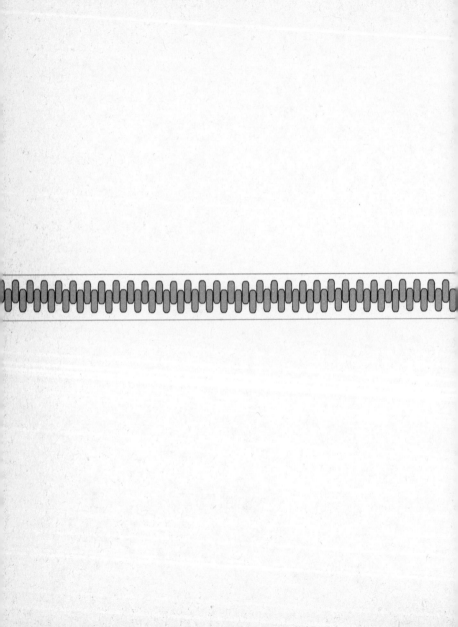

CHAPTER 11

Dealing with Stage Fright, or, Just Shoot Me Now

And he opened the bottomless pit; and there arose a smoke out of the pit, as the smoke of a great furnace; and the sun and the air were darkened by reason of the smoke of the pit.

John Milton

Hell or stage fright? Like it makes a difference—to those who suffer from it, stage fright is hellish indeed.

What scares the pants off you? According to a survey, most people aren't freaked out by classic horror movies, large furry spiders, or even death. Pollsters have discovered that our greatest fear is speaking in front of a group of people. Three-quarters of all Americans admit that they're more afraid of public speaking than death, which means that most people would prefer being *in* the coffin than standing *by* it delivering the eulogy.

The classic advice—*picture the audience naked*—is useless. Why is the image of your boss, your teacher, or complete strangers in the buff supposed to put you at ease? If anything, these images would inspire even more panic. Keep it zipped, fella. In this chapter, you'll learn how to deal with stage fright.

YOU'RE NOT ALONE

Mark Twain spent several days in May, 1901, in Princeton, New Jersey. One evening, he gave a reading in front of a large audience of Princeton students and professors. Twain prefaced his reading by saying:

WORDS UNZIPPED

Glossophobia: Fear of public speaking is so fearful that it even has a medical name. Glossophobia comes from the Greek words for "tongue" and "fear or dread." Sounds about right to us.

I feel exceedingly surreptitious in coming down here without an announcement of any kind. I do not want to see any advertisements around, for the reason that I'm not a lecturer any longer. I reformed long ago, and I break over and commit this sin only just one time this year: and that is moderate, I think, for a person of my disposition. It is not my purpose to lecture any more as long as I live. I never intend to stand up on a platform any more—unless by the request of a sheriff or something like that.

If a public speaker as accomplished as Twain suffered from stage fright, you know you're not alone. Andy Partridge, a new wave musician, said it this way: *I collapsed in France in the middle of a tour. I hadn't been eating properly, I was getting very phobic about audiences, and I collapsed in pure fright.* Jeanne Moreau was typically French in her response to stage fright. She said: *Many people associate stage fright with a fear of looking ridiculous, making a bad impression. For me, it's like a kind of fever. But*

Faith Hill deals with stage fright with that *sang froid* of country singers: *A little bit of stage fright, then I'm ready.*

How do you know if you're suffering from stage fright and not just the flu or some exotic illness like beriberi or crabs? Use this *Stage Fright or Exotic Illness* chart to play do-it-yourself doctor.

Stage Fright	Symptoms of Beriberi, Crabs, or Something from *Alien*?
You have intense anxiety before actually having to speak in public.	No
You have intense anxiety during a public speaking engagement.	No
You avoid events in which you'll be required to speak in front of others.	No
You get nauseous at the thought of giving a speech.	No
You feel shortness of breath at the thought of giving a speech.	No
Your heart rate increases when you give a speech.	No
Your blood pressure soars when you give a speech.	No
Your pupils dilate when you even contemplate giving a speech.	No

Stage Fright	Symptoms of Beriberi, Crabs, or Something from *Alien*?
Your upper neck and back muscles stiffen before and during a speech.	No
Your voice gets tense and quivers when you must give a speech in public.	No
Sometimes you're even totally unable to speak when you must give a speech in public.	No
You hyperventilate when you must give a speech in public.	No
You've actually had a panic attack that mimicked a heart attack when you gave a public speech.	No
You sweat like a horse when you must give a speech in public—even though the room is cold enough to hang meat.	Well, maybe, but some people sweat all the time.

This list of symptoms is fairly depressing. Fortunately, there are some effective ways to deal with stage fright—no creams or ointments involved.

BE PREPARED

The Boy Scouts say it best: Be prepared. Happily, you don't need any merit badges, tents, or knots to conquer stage fright. What you do need is mastery of your material. If you know your speech and feel comfortable with it, your stage fright will decrease. Practice your speech or presentation and revise it until you can present it backwards and forwards. Then prepare a reading copy or notes to bring along, just in case you freeze.

You can reduce stage fright by preparing in other ways as well. Here are some ideas:

- Lay out your clothing, notes, snacks, and so on the night before.
  The more prepared you are, the more relaxed you'll be.

- If it's possible, go to the venue a few days before your speech.

ZIP TIPS

Never apologize for your stage fright. Most of the time, your nervousness doesn't show at all. If you don't say anything about it, few people will notice. If you bring up your nervousness or apologize for any problems you think you'll have with your speech, you're only drawing everyone's attention to it. Zip your lip this time!

If not, arrive at the site with plenty of time to spare. Stroll around the room. Walk from your seat to the place where you'll be speaking. Then stand at the lectern and practice your speech with the microphone.

- Eat.
  If you're nervous, the temptation is to skip food. Don't! Eat something to settle your stomach. Go with whatever sits well in your stomach; most people have good results with tea and toast or other light snacks.

- Be rested.
  Try to sleep well at least a week before a big speech. The less sleep you have, the more apt you are to fall prey to nerves.

- If possible, greet some of the audience members as they arrive.
  Chat with them. It's easier to speak to a group of friends than to a group of strangers. And they'll be more receptive to you, having already met you.

MOVE IT!

A brief workout can also help relieve tension by burning off your excess energy. We're not talking about an hour on the stair master, thigh master, or abs master. That's torture, not exercise. The idea is not to tucker you out completely. The idea is to gently ease some of your tension and get you limbered up. You don't need to break a sweat. Try these ideas:

- Go for a nice stroll.
  Figure about 15 minutes. And resist the temptation to keep walking away from the speech.

- Swing your arms a few times, alternating sides.
  Ditto on your legs.

- Sit comfortably in a straight chair with your back straight.
  Breathe in slowly; hold your breath for 4 to 5 seconds.
  Then slowly exhale.

- To relax your facial muscles, open your mouth and eyes wide and then close them tightly.
  Do this several times.

- Do a few jumping jacks, deep knee bends, and toe touches.
  If this doesn't relax you, at least it will remind you that you can still reach your toes (or that it's time to head to the gym, after you've finished your speech.)

PSYCHE YOURSELF IN . . . NOT OUT

You can psyche yourself out . . . or you can psyche yourself in. Rather than making yourself a basket case, why not imagine the best case scenario? Imagine yourself marching confidently onstage as the audience busts into appreciative applause. Then play out the whole scene. You're speaking clearly and cogently, a master of your domain. Your body language is pitch-perfect. Then comes the end. The audience applauds again, and you stride happily from the stage. People try to shake your hands and throw money and flowers at you.

If you're still feeling shaky, try adopting a *persona*, a different identity. Pretend you're an actor in a play. This may give you the distance you need to feel less nervous. Actors do this all the time to get over stage fright. It works for speakers as well.

IS THE ANSWER IN THE BOTTOM OF THE BOTTLE?

Nope. There are pills that relieve anxiety, lots of them. There's booze, too. But pharmaceuticals and alcohol can have screwy side effects that you can't predict. You never want to end up with your head in your lap because you're stoned on the "little" anxiety reliever your friend/sister/neighbor or even doctor gave you.

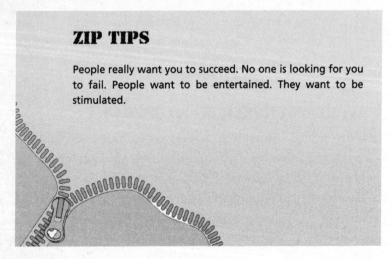

ZIP TIPS

People really want you to succeed. No one is looking for you to fail. People want to be entertained. They want to be stimulated.

RIDE THE WAVE

Everyone feels stage fright. If people deny it, they're fibbing. What happens if you try all the techniques in this chapter, but your stomach still heaves and your hands still shake at the thought of giving a speech? Do what professional speakers do—make your fear work for you. A little bit of stage fright can actually improve your speech by keeping you on edge. The nervous energy and fear that cause stage fright can be an asset to you. Harness these feelings and transform them into vitality and enthusiasm.

Classic actor Eddie Bracken phrased it this way: *But I have fun with the fright, work with it. You have to—that's the timing, that beat of excitement. And when I'm onstage, it's like taking a step into heaven. Poof, you know? Poof—and there I am.*

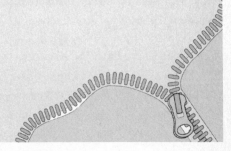

ZIP TIPS

One of the best ways to conquer stage fright is by facing it over and over. The more you speak in public, the more confidence you'll gain.

Stevie Nicks said it like this: *If you have stage fright, it never goes away. But then I wonder: Is the key to that magical performance because of the fear?*

Even the King used this technique to deal with stage fright. Elvis said: *I've never gotten over what they call stage fright. I go through it every show. I'm pretty concerned; I'm pretty much thinking about the show. I never get completely comfortable with it, and I don't let the people around me get comfortable with it, in that I remind them that it's a new crowd out there, it's a new audience, and they haven't seen us before. So it's got to be like the first time we go on.*

PRACTICE SPEECH

Deliver the following speech to an audience—and no, your dog doesn't count. Use the techniques you learned in this chapter to deal with stage fright.

George Graham Vest (1830–1904) was Missouri's U.S. Senator from 1879 to 1903 and became one of the leading public speakers of his time. This speech is from an earlier period in his life when he practiced law in a small Missouri town. Vest delivered the speech while representing a man who sued someone for killing his dog. Vest won the case because of the following speech.

Gentlemen of the Jury: The best friend a man has in the world may turn against him and become his enemy. His son or daughter that he has reared with loving care may prove ungrateful. Those who are nearest and dearest to us, those whom we trust with our happiness and our good name may become traitors to their faith.

The money that a man has, he may lose. It flies away from him, perhaps when he needs it most. A man's reputation may be sacrificed in a moment of ill-considered action. The people who are prone to fall on their knees to do us honor when success is with us, may be the first to throw the stone of malice when failure settles its cloud upon our heads.

The one absolutely unselfish friend that man can have in this selfish world, the one that never deserts him, the one that never proves ungrateful or treacherous is his dog. A man's dog stands by him in prosperity and in poverty, in health and in sickness. He will sleep on the cold ground, where the wintry winds blow and the snow drives fiercely, if only he may be near his master's side. He will kiss the hand that has no food to offer. He will lick the wounds and sores that come in encounters with the roughness of the world. He guards the sleep of his pauper master as if he were a prince. When all other friends desert, he remains. When riches take wings, and reputation falls to pieces, he is as constant in his love as the sun in its journey through the heavens.

If fortune drives the master forth, an outcast in the world, friendless and homeless, the faithful dog asks no higher privilege than that of accompanying him, to guard him against danger, to fight against his enemies. And when the last scene of all comes, and death takes his master in its embrace and his body is laid away in the cold ground, no matter if all other friends pursue their way, there by the graveside will the noble dog be found, his head between his paws, his eyes sad, but open in alert watchfulness, faithful and true even in death.

CHAPTER 12

Moments Like These

ONE OF THE most memorable and dramatic moments in history took place on April 20, 1814, when Napoleon Bonaparte, the Emperor of France, bid farewell to the Old Guard after his failed invasion of Russia and defeat by the Allies. In the courtyard at Fontainebleau, Napoleon said good-bye to the remaining faithful officers of the Old Guard. Here's his speech:

Soldiers of my Old Guard: I bid you farewell. For twenty years I have constantly accompanied you on the road to honor and glory. In these latter times, as in the days of our prosperity, you have invariably been models of courage and fidelity. With men such as you our cause could not be lost; but the war would have been interminable; it would have been civil war, and that would have entailed deeper misfortunes on France.

I have sacrificed all of my interests to those of the country.

I go, but you, my friends, will continue to serve France. Her happiness was my only thought. It will still be the object of my wishes. Do not regret my fate; if I have consented to survive, it is to serve your glory. I intend to write the history of the great achievements we have performed together. Adieu, my friends. Would I could press you all to my heart.

Don't we all wish we could be as eloquent as Napoleon when we leave the stage? Now that you've reached the end of this book, here are the last important things you need to know to make sure that your speeches are as memorable as Napoleon's.

READY FOR YOUR CLOSE-UP? WHEN YOUR SPEECH REALLY STARTS

Take this quick quiz. When does your speech really start?

[ ] When you start speaking

[ ] When you arrive at the podium

[ ] When you walk into the room

Your speech begins when you walk into the room. That's because your audience starts judging you the moment they see you—even if you're not scheduled to start speaking until much later in the program. The way you walk into the room telegraphs your control of the situation, so be sure to walk in with confidence.

Q & A

So your speech is over and you're holding a question-and-answer session. It's a good way to get feedback, but it can be a minefield because, unlike your speech, you've got no control over what you can be asked. Or do you?

One great way to keep a handle on the question part of a Q & A is to have people write their questions on index cards. You then collect the cards and read the ones you want. Or, you can have an assistant screen the questions as he or she collects the cards and hand you the ones you're most likely to want to answer.

If you do take questions from the floor, follow these top ten guidelines.

1. Rephrase the question in your own words to make sure you understand it.

2. If you still don't get what the person is asking, be sure to ask for clarification. Never answer anything you don't understand.

3. Make sure that everyone in the audience has heard the question before you answer it.

4. If one person asks multiple questions in a row, separate the questions and answer them one at a time, in the order in which they were asked.

5. Answer briefly but completely.

6. Keep your cool, no matter how riled you may feel.

7. Nonetheless, feel free to cut someone off who is trying to manipulate the discussion, hog the floor, or embarrass you.

8. Try to avoid humorous responses, unless you've been hired as a comedian.

9. If you want to hold a Q & A but fear that no one will ask any questions, plant a few friends in the audience to ask the first few questions. This should get the ball rolling.

10. Don't be afraid to say "I don't know" if you don't know the answer to a question. Never try to fake your way through it with false, misleading, or empty information.

Remember, no matter what you're asked, you're not obligated to answer any question you don't want to answer. You can simply say, "I'd rather not comment on that issue right now," or "I'll take a pass on that question," or "I'll have to get back to you on that." If you do offer to "Get back to you on that," be sure that you do. Your credibility depends on it.

WELL, IT'S NOT OVER 'TIL IT'S OVER

When your speech and the Q & A are over, don't dash from the podium. Stay. Graciously acknowledge the applause and

- Thank the audience for their attention.

- Gather your notes, if you have any.
  This will keep your hands busy for a few moments.

- Walk away with a firm step.
  Remember, people are still staring at you.

- Sit down in the audience or wherever a chair has been provided for you.

- Sit quietly through the rest of the speakers.

LEARN FROM YOUR TRIUMPHS AND TRAGEDIES

After your speech, praise yourself for what you did well, but don't beat yourself up for what didn't go as smoothly. Instead, learn from your missteps. Do a frank assessment of the speech and work on the areas that need improvement. Sometimes, the areas are out of your control—a tornado hits the building during your speech, for instance—but other times, you can rehearse more, make more eye contact, or speak more slowly.

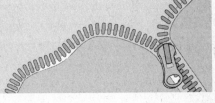

ZIP TIPS

If people in the audience are being rude, pause and wait a moment for the cell phone conversation, rustling, or talking to end. If you're getting heckled and the heckler won't stop, pause and ask your host to remove the jerk. All speakers deserve basic politeness.

PRACTICE SPEECH

One more chance to practice. Here's a speech from William Lyon Phelps (1865–1943), an American educator, literary critic, and author. Phelps delivered this speech in response to the Nazis burning books on May 10, 1933. Now that you've finished this book, you're reminded once again of the importance of books to civilization.

The habit of reading is one of the greatest resources of mankind; and we enjoy reading books that belong to us much more than if they are borrowed. A borrowed book is like a guest in the house; it must be treated with punctiliousness, with a certain considerate formality. You must see that it sustains no damage; it must not suffer while under your roof. You cannot leave it carelessly, you cannot mark it, you cannot turn down the pages, you cannot use it familiarly. And then, some day, although this is seldom done, you really ought to return it.

But your own books belong to you; you treat them with that affectionate intimacy that annihilates formality. Books are for use, not for show; you should own no book that you are afraid to mark up, or afraid to place on the table, wide open and face down. A good reason for marking favorite passages in books is that this practice enables you to remember more easily the significant sayings, to refer to them quickly, and then in later years, it is like visiting a forest where you once blazed a trail. You have the pleasure of going over the old ground, and recalling both the intellectual scenery and your own earlier self.

Everyone should begin collecting a private library in youth; the instinct of private property, which is fundamental in human beings, can here be cultivated with every advantage and no evils. One should have one's own bookshelves, which should not have doors, glass windows, or keys; they should be free and accessible to the hand as well as to the eye. The best of mural decorations is books; they are more varied in color and appearance than any wallpaper, they are more attractive in design, and they have the prime advantage of being separate personalities, so that if you sit alone in the room in the firelight, you are surrounded with intimate friends. The knowledge that they are there in plain view is both stimulating and refreshing. You do not have to read them all. Most of my indoor life is spent in a room containing six thousand books; and I have a stock answer to the invariable question that comes from strangers "Have you read all of these books?"

"Some of them twice." This reply is both true and unexpected.

There are of course no friends like living, breathing, corporeal men and women; my devotion to reading has never made me a recluse. How could it? Books are of the people, by the people, for the people. Literature is the immortal part of history; it is the best and most enduring part of personality. But book-friends have this advantage over living friends; you can enjoy the most truly aristocratic society in the world whenever you want it. The great dead are beyond our physical reach, and the great living are usually almost as inaccessible; as for our personal friends and acquaintances, we cannot always see them. Perchance they are asleep, or away on a journey. But in a private library, you can at any moment converse with Socrates or Shakespeare or Carlyle or Dumas or Dickens or Shaw or Barrie or Galsworthy. And there is no doubt that in these books you see these men at their best. They wrote for you. They "laid themselves out," they did their ultimate best to entertain you, to make a favorable impression. You are as necessary to them as an audience is to an actor; only instead of seeing them masked, you look into their innermost heart of heart.

NOTES UNZIPPED

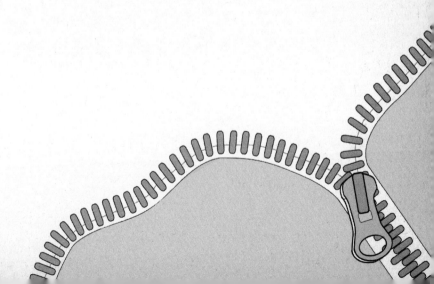

NOTES UNZIPPED

NOTES UNZIPPED

NOTES UNZIPPED

GIVE US YOUR FEEDBACK

Peterson's, a Nelnet company, publishes a full line of resources to help guide you through the college admission process. Peterson's publications can be found at your local bookstore, library, and high school guidance office, and you can access us online at www.petersons.com.

We welcome any comments or suggestions you may have about this publication and invite you to complete our online survey at www.petersons.com/booksurvey. Or you can fill out the paper survey on the next page, tear it out, and mail it to us at:

Publishing Department
Peterson's
2000 Lenox Drive
Lawrenceville, NJ 08648

Peterson's
Book Satisfaction Survey

Give Us Your Feedback

Thank you for choosing Peterson's as your source for personalized solutions for your education and career achievement. Please take a few minutes to answer the following questions. Your answers will go a long way in helping us to produce the most user-friendly and comprehensive resources to meet your individual needs.

When completed, please tear out this page and mail it to us at:

> Publishing Department
> Peterson's, a Nelnet company
> 2000 Lenox Drive
> Lawrenceville, NJ 08648

You can also complete this survey online at **www.petersons.com/booksurvey.**

1. What is the ISBN of the book you have purchased? (The ISBN can be found on the book's back cover in the lower right-hand corner.) _____

2. Where did you purchase this book?
- ❏ Retailer, such as Barnes & Noble
- ❏ Online reseller, such as Amazon.com
- ❏ Petersons.com
- ❏ Other (please specify) _____

3. If you purchased this book on Petersons.com, please rate the following aspects of your online purchasing experience on a scale of 4 to 1 (4 = Excellent and 1 = Poor).

	4	3	2	1
Comprehensiveness of Peterson's Online Bookstore page	❏	❏	❏	❏
Overall online customer experience	❏	❏	❏	❏

4. Which category best describes you?
- ❏ High school student
- ❏ Parent of high school student
- ❏ College student
- ❏ Graduate/professional student
- ❏ Returning adult student
- ❏ Teacher
- ❏ Counselor
- ❏ Working professional/military
- ❏ Other (please specify) _____

5. Rate your overall satisfaction with this book.

Extremely Satisfied	Satisfied	Not Satisfied
❏	❏	❏

6. Rate each of the following aspects of this book on a scale of 4 to 1 (4 = Excellent and 1 = Poor).

	4	3	2	1
Comprehensiveness of the information	❏	❏	❏	❏
Accuracy of the information	❏	❏	❏	❏
Usability	❏	❏	❏	❏
Cover design	❏	❏	❏	❏
Book layout	❏	❏	❏	❏
Special features (e.g., CD, flashcards, charts, etc.)	❏	❏	❏	❏
Value for the money	❏	❏	❏	❏

7. This book was recommended by:
- ❏ Guidance counselor
- ❏ Parent/guardian
- ❏ Family member/relative
- ❏ Friend
- ❏ Teacher
- ❏ Not recommended by anyone—I found the book on my own
- ❏ Other (please specify) _____

8. Would you recommend this book to others?

Yes	Not Sure	No
❏	❏	❏

9. Please provide any additional comments.

_____

_____

_____

_____

_____

Remember, you can tear out this page and mail it to us at:

> Publishing Department
> Peterson's, a Nelnet company
> 2000 Lenox Drive
> Lawrenceville, NJ 08648

or you can complete the survey online at **www.petersons.com/booksurvey.**

Your feedback is important to us at Peterson's, and we thank you for your time!

If you would like us to keep in touch with you about new products and services, please include your e-mail address here: _____